PRAISE FOR CONVERSATIONS WITH RODNEY

"From the time I had the privilege to meet Mr. Rodney Flowers I was overwhelmed with his desires to live life as if his life was never impacted. It was refreshing to see someone live through and with an altered life instead of using it as a crutch to get sympathy. Rodney's new book, <u>Conversations with Rodney: Unchained Breaking Free from Your Own Prison</u>, allows me to chart through every month and find a new reason to keep pushing. As someone who lives with an illness I read this book with anticipation for each month so I can be renewed, if you will, with a refreshed sense of purpose. Thank you Rodney for your transparency and your determination."

—**Ivy N. McQuain, MBA,** owner of BLI Publishing

"International bestselling author Rodney Flowers, "The Get Up" guy, has quickly established himself as a global inspirational thought leader and authority on digging deep within to find your own personal power. This book is a testament to his genuine commitment to help people in all walks of life. When it comes to *overcoming adversity, Rodney has done what most would have considered unthinkable not to mention impossible. In his latest book, <u>Conversations with Rodney – Unchained: Breaking Free of Your Own Prisons</u>, he addresses in a month-by-month study format, the 12 most common types of questions he is asked, sharing the wisdom of his responses based on his own personal experiences and achievements. As a result, he inspires his readers to grit up, make decisions to set meaningful goals, to never quit thus uplifting their belief in their ability to accomplish anything. The results ultimately change lives. Forever."*

—**Carolyn Flower,** President of Flower Communications Enterprises and Author of *Gravitate 2 Gratitude – Journal Your Journey (Begin Within)*

CONVERSATIONS WITH **RODNEY**

VOLUME 1

UNCHAINED: BREAKING FREE OF YOUR OWN PRISONS

RODNEY C. FLOWERS

Published by
Hasmark Publishing
http://www.hasmarkpublishing.com

Copyright © 2015 Rodney Flowers All Rights Reserved.

No part of this book may be reproduced or transmitted in any form or by any means, electronic or mechanical, including photocopying, recording or by any information storage and retrieval system, without written permission from the author, except for the inclusion of brief quotations in a review.

Disclaimer: This book is designed to provide information and motivation to our readers. It is sold with the understanding that the publisher is not engaged to render any type of psychological, legal, or any other kind of professional advice. The content of each article is the sole expression and opinion of its author, and not necessarily that of the publisher. No warranties or guarantees are expressed or implied by the publisher's choice to include any of the content in this volume. Neither the publisher nor the individual author(s) shall be liable for any physical, psychological, emotional, financial, or commercial damages, including, but not limited to, special, incidental, consequential or other damages. Our views and rights are the same: You are responsible for your own choices, actions, and results.

All Scripture quotations are taken from King James Version of the Bible.

Permission should be addressed in writing to: Rodney Flowers, PO Box 1308, Leonardtown, MD 20650 or Rodney@RodneyFlowers.com

Editor, Stephanie Clark
http://CLWritingServices.com

Cover Design, JESH Art Studios

Layout, DocUmeant Designs
www.DocUmeantDesigns.com

Photos, E&R Photography
www.EandRphotography.smugmug.com

First Edition, 2016

ISBN-13: 978-1-988071-15-2
ISBN-10: 1988071151

CONTENTS

FOREWORD..V
INTRODUCTION IX

CHAPTER 1
      JANUARY: ALWAYS WIN 1
      Conclusion.........................12

CHAPTER 2
      FEBRUARY: OVERESTIMATING THE
      IMPORTANCE OF INTELLIGENCE 15
      Conclusion.........................21

CHAPTER 3
      MARCH: YOU ARE NOT A QUITTER! 23
      Conclusion.........................28

CHAPTER 4
      APRIL: THE NEW LEAF AND THE CREATOR 31
      Conclusion.........................37

CHAPTER 5
      MAY: BELIEVE ... YOU HAVE WHAT
      IT TAKES 39
      Conclusion.........................44

CHAPTER 6
- JUNE: GROW UP 47
- Conclusion 51

CHAPTER 7
- JULY: FOLLOW YOUR HEART WITH PASSION 53
- Conclusion 58

CHAPTER 8
- AUGUST: CHANGE REQUIRES CHANGE .. 61
- Conclusion 66

CHAPTER 9
- SEPTEMBER: FAITH MATTERS 69
- Conclusion 74

CHAPTER 10
- OCTOBER: MINDSET 75
- Conclusion 80

CHAPTER 11
- NOVEMBER: PERSPECTIVE IS EVERYTHING 83
- Conclusion 88

CHAPTER 12
- DECEMBER: IT'S NEVER TOO LATE TO DREAM 89
- Conclusion 94

AFTERWORD 97
ABOUT THE AUTHOR 99

FOREWORD

Life is a miraculous journey that requires a courageous heart and spirit to traverse the jagged edges of our painful experiences, and receive the abundant joy that's waiting for us right around the corner. Both joy and heartache help us to grow and stretch physically, spiritually, and psychologically, because we would not know one without the other as you'll see in Rodney's thoroughly thought-out answers in his book Conversations with Rodney . . .

When Rodney asked me to write the foreword, I read and thoroughly thought about the questions included in this book and how they can lead each one of us to a deeper truth of who we are and embrace our higher purpose. As a licensed Psychotherapist, I've listened to hundreds of stories and have come to the realization that the answers we seek lie in the questions we ask ourselves and how we answer those questions given where we are in our psychological and spiritual development. As Leo Babauta said, *"At the end of the day, the questions we ask of ourselves determine the type of people that we will become."*

In this collection of 12 conversations, Rodney responds from a strength-based perspective that enhances and equips us to overcome the taxing circumstances and barriers we face in life, and experience a deeper sense of joy. From this point of view Rodney also encourages psychological, cognitive, social, and emotional growth via impactful and enlightening insights that are geared towards the following:

- Boosting self-love and self confidence
- Igniting the fire within us to "Get Up and Grit Up"
- Building meaningful relationships
- Developing a mindset of peace and joy, and a sense of understanding
- Increasing our faith and understanding of our responsibility towards success

Throughout the past two decades as a successful CEO of a counseling and coaching business, one thing has become crystal clear: All of us have the same basic wants and needs. We all have the same questions, same struggles, and same ambition to live a successful, peaceful and joyful life.

Over the years I have gotten to know thousands of people from different ethnic backgrounds, from different cities and countries, who live at various socioeconomic levels. What do we all have in common? Every one of us yearns for acceptance, love, happiness, fulfillment, and hope for a better future. The way we pursue these needs are different for each us, but the fundamentals are the same as Rodney so eloquently addresses in this book

The strength exuberated in this book is so powerful the reader will feel Rodney's passion to lead and influence others to Never Give Up. Life can be tough, but we're not victims. We have a choice to saddle up and drive our own bus or have someone else drive it for us. Rodney, who was never supposed to walk again after a football accident that left him paralyzed from the neck down, made the choice to GET UP and drive his own bus. He chose to embrace his life and inspire others to get up, grit up and get all that is theirs for the taking in this world.

As a therapist, it is very clear to me that the questions and answers contained in this book will help us to embrace the sacrifices it takes to get us where we want to go, and motivate us to focus on the next steps we need to take to move toward our passions and dreams. Questions like, "What do you do when you're feeling hopeless from failing to reach childhood goals and dreams? What do you do when you feel you do not possess the intelligence to be what you desire to be? And what do you do when you have difficulty believing in your ability to reach your goals?", and many more. The thought-provoking answers will challenge you to dig deeper into your soul and cultivate your true calling that will ultimately lead you to success.

Life's answers come to us in many forms. Rodney was the answer to my prayer, and my question of, "What's next?". When I met him, I was seeking my next step. I was fed up and feeling lost. Then came Rodney with his charm, determination, upbeat nature, and deep sense of passion to inspire, encourage, and motivate others to live better lives. I found myself inspired and exhilarated to change what was not working, and seek new ways of delivering my messages. No matter what questions you have, whether it's finding your life's meaning, feeling stuck, feeling like a failure, or struggling with how to become successful, Rodney addresses all these issues in Conversations with Rodney.

> "It's a funny thing about life; if you refuse to accept anything but the best, you very often get it."
> W. Somerset Maugham

Whether you browse through this book, or read it from cover to cover, you will find yourself more inspired, more determined, more cognizant of the gifts you possess, and more thoughtful with every page. Most of all, you will want to sit face to face with Rodney and have more conversation.

From my own personal experience, I am confident that when you have finished this book you will experience a sense of peace, clarity, and a knowing that you are one of those people who are prepared for all opportunities that await you in this life. The knowledge you will gain from the conversations herein will yield huge dividends for yourself, and empower you to live the highest and grandest expression of yourself.

Dr. Sithembile (Stem) Mahlatini, Ed.D., LICSW
Licensed Psychotherapist and Certified Professional Coach

INTRODUCTION

Recently I was asked what I would put in a letter if I could send it back through time and deliver it to myself on my 13th birthday. The question was posed in a cavalier manner—I believe the asker intended it to be a mildly interesting conversation starter as opposed to an invitation to some deep, soul-baring discussion—and I quickly rattled off a pithy response.

However, later that evening, I started really considering the passage of time in our lives and the opportunities we have each and every day. Some days we make the best choice and seize advantage of the time we have here; other days, it seems that our choices are not so good and lead to wasted time and effort at best.

I began considering all of the people who have come to me for advice. Generally, I find that people who come to me fall into one of two categories: either they desire to make a change and are afraid to try, or they have some great regret that now holds them back from moving forward with their lives. Both categories of people can be greatly helped by reading my book *Essential Assertions* and following the advice and suggestions therein.

However, I'm aware that some people are very busy and they don't want or need a one-size-fits all answer to their questions. If I were to simply respond to everyone with, "Read *Essential Assertions,*" I would doubtless help some people while disappointing others. Although the advice in that book is something that I believe can help people from all walks and all stages of life, I thought I would put together something a little bit shorter and highlight the types of issues I see most frequently.

This book is a collection of the 12 types of questions I see most often, along with a short discussion of my response to each type. While your question might vary in the details, chances are if you have something to ask me it will fall into one of these 12 categories of questions.

A great way to use this book is to spend one month on each chapter. The chapters are short enough that you can easily read a chapter in a single day, so you may want to read the chapter on the first day of the month and then spend some time reviewing it and applying the principles laid out in my answer to your own situation.

In all of the advice I give here, if I had to pick one underlying principle to stress as fundamental above all others, it would be the principle of determining within yourself that you will not quit no matter what happens. The decision that you are going to grit up and keep working towards your goal—regardless of the cost; regardless of the number of times you fall down—is the single most important factor in your eventual success.

> *"Fight one more round. When your arms are so tired that you can hardly lift your hands to come on guard, fight one more round. When your nose is bleeding and your eyes are black and you are so tired that you wish your opponent would crack you one on the jaw and put you to sleep, fight one more round—remembering that the man who always fights one more round is never whipped."*
>
> — James Corbett

To this end, I have chosen my favorite quote out of all the ones I use in this book to cite here.

This quote, I believe, embodies the determination and drive I would like to impart to you, dear reader. No matter what happens during your journey through life, if you set your mind to it, you will be able to overcome adversity. Everything else is simply details. The number one requirement for success is simply the will to be successful and the determination to move relentlessly and inexorably towards your goal regardless of the challenges you encounter.

Enjoy your journey, and remember that the greatest tool you have at your disposal is your mind and your will. Once you determine to accomplish your goal, nothing will be able to stop you!

Here's to you, and your continued success!

Rodney

CHAPTER 1

JANUARY: ALWAYS WIN

Question: For several years I have been dissatisfied with my situation in life. Without going into too much detail, I will just say that when I was younger, I had certain goals I wanted to achieve. I tried to reach these goals but failed. Since then, I occasionally think about my unrealized goals and how nice it would be to see them become reality, but I don't have the strength to try again because the disappointment I felt was so crushing that I really don't want to take the chance on experiencing that again. I would like to be able to move past the disappointment of my failure, but I feel like it is pointless to even try because I am the way I am, and it seems that nothing is going to change that. Do you have any advice for me?

Well, first I would say that you haven't failed. If you read my book Essential Assertions, you will see that I devote a significant amount of one chapter discussing what happens when the results are something other than what you planned for. And, so long as you gave 100% and learned something from it, I would say it is incorrect to classify it as a failure.

Second, I have an expression I like to use: grit up. I will explain it more in-depth below, but for now, I would encourage you to pick yourself up and keep trying—no matter what—until you reach your goal.

Third, I want to encourage you to keep moving towards your goal, but don't just look at the end achievement; rather, take some time to focus on the smaller victories along the way and celebrate them as well. If you take care of the smaller steps along the way, the big goal will take care of itself.

Finally, I want to point out that very little in life that is worth anything is obtained without taking a chance. If something is worth having, more likely than not it is going to require that you take some chances to get it.

> *"I have not failed 700 times. I have not failed once. I have succeeded in proving that those 700 ways will not work. When I have eliminated the ways that will not work, I will find the way that will work."*
>
> — Thomas Edison

Thomas Edison. What do you think of when you hear the name? Someone working with a little glass bulb containing a filament inside, hoping it would someday light up? Someone working on a machine that could record sounds and play them back? Someone who was brilliant and one of the sharpest minds of our time?

Undeniably, Edison was all these things. But you know what I think of when I hear his name? I think of the above quote. Edison was someone who did not ever say "I failed." You know why? Because he never did fail.

So, you may be wondering, *Rodney, are you crazy? If he wanted to harness electricity to produce a working light bulb, unless it worked exactly as he planned the first time—which of course we know is not true—then by definition he failed.*

My response would be, "Nope. He did not fail. Not even one time." You see, many of us have an incorrect definition of the word *fail.* To get results other than the ones you were expecting is not necessarily a failure. For example, if you try to build a rocket ship and it blows up on the launch pad, obviously that's not the result you were expecting. *But it is not necessarily a failure.*

Let us redefine what it is to fail. To fail is (1) to get results other than what you want because you did not give yourself 100% to it; and (2) to learn nothing from the results. If you put everything you have into reaching your goal and you don't quite get what you were planning or expecting, that doesn't mean it was a failure. If you took something away from the experience—something that helped you to get better and come one step closer to reaching your ultimate goal—then it is not a failure.

To fail is to put in a half-hearted effort and learn nothing from your results. If you are trying to build a rocket ship and you just kind of toss the ingredients for the fuel together and—when it inevitably explodes on the launch pad—you just wander away to play video games without bothering to investigate the wreckage and find out *why it exploded,* then yes, I would say that's a failure.

On the other hand, if you carefully and meticulously craft your rocket ship, documenting all the steps and recording precisely every action you take, then when it blows up you spend time investigating the matter and learning what went wrong so you can avoid that in the future, then *it is not a failure.* A goal is reached in incremental steps. Arguably, this involves many steps that you must take without incident in order to reach the final goal. So if you spend time and energy learning how *not to misstep*, then it's not a failure; rather, it is a necessary part of the learning process.

So, let's address your initial statement "I tried to reach these goals but failed." I would ask you: Did you *really* fail? Did you give it your best effort and—if so—did you learn what *doesn't work?* I would say that you definitely learned something *not to do* and—once you have eliminated all the things you should not do—you will eventually have a clear path between where you are and where you wish to be.

Achieving an outcome which was not what you desired is not a failure so long as you put your best effort into it and take something away from the experience; rather, it is simply a part of the learning process. Let me encourage you right now to take what you learned from your experience, pick yourself up off the ground, and get back to work. That leads to our next point.

> "The spirit, the will to win, and the will to excel are the things that endure. These qualities are so much more important than the events that occur."
> — Vince Lombardi

I chose these quotes because they display a quality I like to refer to as grit. Grit is that dogged determination that rests deep within a man (or woman) which insists on trying again, and again, and again no matter what happens. Grit is the will to persevere—regardless of the circumstances—and to continue persevering until you reach your goal. Grit is the fire that burns within the furnace of your heart; that fire which drives you on towards greatness.

What is it that makes someone great? Is it intelligence? Talent? Education? I would submit that while these matters may certainly help, they alone are insufficient. I played football when I was younger and I saw firsthand examples of wasted talent. Athletes who possessed the ability to be great, but failed to reach that greatness because their work ethic was lacking. Likewise, in the United States today, you need not look very far to find someone who is very highly educated and yet has failed to accomplish much with his or her life. And intelligence? In my experience a high level of intelligence can actually handicap someone from going far in life because he or she gets used to relying on that intelligence to get by and—when he or she inevitably reaches the point where raw intelligence alone no longer cuts it—he or she simply gives up because the notion of hard work is so foreign.

I would submit that what makes someone great is the grit they have. The grit to pick themselves up once they've fallen to the mat, wipe the blood off their face, and once again join the fray. The grit to resolve deep within yourself that—no matter what—you simply will not be denied your goal. The grit to continue fighting regardless of how many times you've tried before.

The grit you have is more important that the outward results of your attempts. As Vince Lombardi said, your will to excel is more important than the events that have occurred. Why is this? Because, if the only thing that matters is what occurs when you try, then serendipity will play a greater role in your success in life than anything else. You will either succeed or not based purely on the outcome of your haphazard attempts.

But this, as we all can attest, is simply not the case. What matters is your determination to keep going. To keep working. To keep searching, searching, searching for the way to reach the destination you have in mind. If one thing doesn't work, you take what you learned and you go back to the drawing board. And you try again. If you have no will to excel, then you will be finished as soon as your initial attempt falls short—and it almost certainly will, as very few goals are achieved on the first attempt.

> *"Fight one more round. When your arms are so tired that you can hardly lift your hands to come on guard, fight one more round. When your nose is bleeding and your eyes are black and you are so tired that you wish your opponent would crack you one on the jaw and put you to sleep, fight one more round—remembering that the man who always fights one more round is never whipped."*
>
> James Corbett

> *Nothing in the world can take the place of persistence. Talent will not; nothing is more common than unsuccessful men with talent. Genius will not; unrewarded genius is almost a proverb. Education alone will not; the world is full of educated derelicts. Persistence and determination alone are omnipotent. The slogan 'press on' has solved and always will solve the problems of the human race.*
>
> —John Calvin Coolidge

Let me add another quote here, one that I have found to be particularly fitting when it comes to the elements of success:

This demonstrates exactly what I'm talking about; *pressing on*. Having the grit and determination to go at it yet again. To keep working—keep innovating—until you get to where you want to be. Press on, and do not count the times you have fallen short. Press on, and only look forward toward your goal. Press on, and let others waste their time and energy shaking their heads and proclaiming, "It's no use." One day you will stand triumphantly over your conquered obstacle while they will still be in the exact same place where they started. But you will never get there unless you have the grit to keep going regardless of how difficult the path may seem.

When you fall down yet again, then it's time for you to get up—or grit up as I like to say—roll up your sleeves, and redouble your efforts. You must determine deep within your being that you will not be denied. You may not accomplish what you are looking to accomplish time, after time, after time, but that will not deter you from gritting up and trying again.

Each time you put your shoulder once more to the plow and begin to push you will find that you have added a piece to the puzzle. You will have discovered—if nothing else—something new that does not work, so you can then eliminate that something from your formula. Once you have eliminated all the ways that do not work, you will be left with the solution, which brings us to our next point:

I want to spend a few moments talking with you about the importance of the little steps along the way. Sometimes people will set a goal for themselves, and that's good. But if the goal is a lofty, ambitious one—as it should be—it can be easy to get so caught up in the achievement of that one goal that everything else along the way gets disregarded.

This is a mistake, because you will never arrive at your ultimate goal without many intermediate steps along the way. Let's again take the illustration of building a rocket ship. If you set this as your goal, and if this is the only thing you can see, you may find yourself up against a wall with no way to proceed.

In order to have a rocket ship, you need an engine. You need life-support systems. You need control mechanisms. You need all sorts of things. And you can break that down even further: before you can have an engine you need a fuel source, a method of transferring the fuel to the combustion chamber, a way to ignite the fuel, a way to direct the controlled explosion that occurs inside the combustion chamber, and so on. Every goal is composed of many separate steps; if you only look at the end goal and overlook the separate steps you may have a difficult time arriving there.

In addition, if you overlook the intermediate steps, you will miss out on a great deal of joy, satisfaction, and the sense of accomplishment you get when you do reach a goal. Using the rocket ship illustration, it is quite an achievement to create an engine capable of lifting a machine off the ground. So, when you have reached this stage—the stage where your engine is performing as needed—that in itself is cause for celebration. Sure, perhaps you're not quite ready to fly yet, but you are one step closer than you were!

In reaching your goal, you will take many steps. Each step gets you closer to the end result; each step is in itself an accomplishment. So you should take the time to celebrate each step. Each step is actually required to get to the end result, so in a sense, the achievement of each individual step is just as important as the final step. Consider, in a journey of 1,000 miles, if you refuse to go the 325th mile, then you'll never get to mile 326, and then you'll never get to 327, and so on. So each individual step of the process is crucial to the achievement of your end goal. For this reason, you should not develop tunnel vision to the extent that you see only your ultimate goal; instead, celebrate as each stage along the way is completed.

The flip side of this is to remember that it takes thousands of steps to move a mile. So, while each step moves you closer towards your ultimate goal, don't spend too much time resting on your laurels and celebrating every time you take another step. If you do this, you'll spend too much time celebrating and not enough time looking ahead to your goal.

The aim here is to be balanced: do not neglect the significance of accomplishing a single step along your journey; at the same time, do not overemphasize each single step you take because to do so will result in premature celebration and an excess use of your time and energy on celebrating.

Your journey will be a long and arduous one. You should keep your spirit buoyed by considering the significance of how far you have already come; at the same time, each time you take a step and get a little bit closer to your end destination, remember that you still have a long way to go. Don't be discouraged by how far you have to go, but neither should you be so overjoyed at the few steps that you've already taken that you abandon sight of your end result.

Celebrate your accomplishments—especially those small, intermediate steps without which you would never reach your goal—but never be content until you finally arrive at your ultimate destination. Then, and only then, may you sit back and say "I did it!" Put differently, celebrate each individual step as a way of keeping your spirits up, but at the same time don't let the inner fire die down until you have reached your ultimate goal. You must determine within yourself to keep pressing on, day by day, step by step, until at long last you have your ultimate goal in your hands.

For my final point, I want to talk with you about taking calculated risks:

Do you want to accomplish nothing with your life? If so, here's the best way to get there: sit tight where it's safe and never take any risks whatsoever. If you never take any risks, then you'll arrive, safe and sound, at the conclusion of your life. And you'll have nothing to show for your time on this earth.

Can a bird fly without spreading its wings and launching itself into space? Can a person run without taking the risk of stubbing his or her toe or tripping over something? Can you warm yourself by a fire without striking a match and setting something alight? Can an opera singer sing a song without running the chance that his or her voice may crack and warble? Of course the answer is "no" to all of these questions. And here we come to a principle that is well worth remembering: Nothing that is worthwhile can be gained or achieved without some measure of risk.

Consider history, and look at some of the greatest accomplishments and inventions. Were they seized without the undertaking of some measure of risk? The invention of gunpowder, the harnessing of electricity, the development of nuclear power, mechanized flight, ocean crossings, deep-sea exploration, the moon landing, travel by automobile, and so on. The list goes on and on, and one thing every single item has in common is this: every single one of them is not without risk, especially to those person(s) who pioneered the way for the rest of us to follow.

Consider if Columbus (or the Vikings, depending on which version of history you subscribe to) had never set out to cross the Atlantic Ocean, opting instead to cling to the shorelines of their respective countries? Or what if the Wright Brothers decided to stay on the ground where it was safe? What if—as some people argued for—automobiles were never developed because it was too dangerous to move any faster than the speed of a horse? Where would we, as a society be today were it not for the great visionaries and risk-takers of the past?

You mention in your question that you don't want to take a chance on experiencing disappointment again, but what will you do with your life if you are afraid to take any chances? Everything you do in life that is worthwhile will involve some element of risk. Because of this, the presence of risk alone should not be enough to deter you from endeavoring to reach your goals.

Now let me be clear: I am not saying that you should completely disregard all risk and press on blindly no matter the cost. To do so would be foolhardy and invite disaster. No, what I am saying is that some degree of risk is inevitable when it comes to accomplishing anything of any importance; the key, then, is to act prudently to minimize the degree of risk which is posed by a given course of action to the best of your ability while acknowledging at the same time that some element of risk will always be present and will not be enough to cause you to divert your course of action.

There is nothing at all wrong with taking steps to minimize your exposure to risk *so long as you do not become so risk averse that you abandon your plans entirely.* You must find a balance between minimizing your exposure to risk and being willing to roll the dice and take a chance. There is a balance to be adhered to here, and straying too much to either extreme—being completely risk averse or acting with complete disregard of all elements of risk—can delay or even halt altogether your progress towards your goal.

Take too much risk unnecessarily and you may find that your endeavors end in ruin; avoid all elements of risk completely and you will find that you never go anywhere or accomplish anything worthwhile. The key is to strike a balance between the two.

I am not too concerned here about counseling you on how to avoid unnecessary risks; for most of us, it is hardwired into us to be risk averse, and only a very few brave (and foolhardy) souls can truly say that they have no consideration whatsoever about the risk involved with their decisions. For this reason, I do not intend to spend much time encouraging you to avoid unnecessary risks: the chances are overwhelmingly in favor of you doing that without any prompting from me.

Rather, I am more concerned with counseling you to accept that some degree of risk is inevitable and cannot be avoided if you have any hope of accomplishing anything worthwhile with your life. You must learn to accept that risk is simply a part of life and—while it is prudent to minimize risk as much as possible—risk should not be minimized to the point where it diminishes your chances of success.

The less risk a choice entails, the less reward it usually brings with it. This principle is repeated over and over in many aspects of our daily lives. Nowhere is it more crystal clear than in the matter of investing in various securities on the stock market. Those instruments which are deemed to have a higher risk well of necessity have to pay out higher returns in order to capture investor dollars; on the other hand, those instruments which are deemed to be completely safe will always bring in the lowest returns.

The key for you is determining what is the optimal balance of risk vs. reward in your life. Every person is different and every person has a different level of risk tolerance. To an extent, this is a good thing, as it is highly unlikely that someone with no regard whatsoever for risk would ever amount to anything; on the other hand, when taken too far, the desire to avoid risk can seriously hamstring you in life.

So, although there is always a risk that you run, I want to encourage you to press on towards your goal regardless. In your case the risk seems to be relatively minor: you run the risk of achieving an outcome other than what you set out to achieve and having to deal with some bitter disappointment as a result. From what you have told me I do not believe that this risk should be enough to give you pause when you are considering your actions. First, it is not like you are running the risk of losing life or limb should something unexpected happen; second, as we have discussed above, so long as you truly give everything you have towards achieving your goal—and so long as you learn something from the outcome—then it is not a failure anyway, even if you do not achieve the outcome you are hoping for.

Standing from the point of view that you truly cannot fail regardless of the outcome of your actions, and remembering that nothing worthwhile is accomplished without some degree of risk, I want to encourage you to grit up, dust off your hands, and get back to work accomplishing your dreams and goals.

Conclusion

I want to encourage you to redefine your definition of the word *fail*. If you set out to achieve something and you truly give your best effort towards your goal it is not a failure if you achieve an outcome other than the one for which you were aiming. So long as you learned something from the experience which you can then apply towards your next attempt then it is not a failure; rather, it is simply a step in the process which gave you valuable information to be used when you ultimately do accomplish your goal. You have not failed; instead, you have discovered a method which does not work and you can now eliminate that method from your list of alternatives. Once you have eliminated all the ways that will not work, you will be left with the way that works. Thus you have not failed.

I want to encourage you to reach deep within yourself and find the grit there. The grit within you is that quality which will never say die; that quality which will push you to get up again, and again, and again, and keep working towards your goal until you finally reach it. Grit is the fire that burns within you which refuses to be quenched by the waters of a temporary setback; it burns within you and pushes you far past the point where other people would have given up because you know—deep within your being—that you can and will accomplish your goal. It is simply a matter of getting up and trying again until you do.

At the same time, I want to encourage you to take a few moments along the way and celebrate the accomplishments that you have already achieved. Remember that you cannot walk 1,000 miles without first taking a step, and then another, and then another, and so on. Every step that you take in your journey is a necessary part of the completion of that journey. Do not discount the importance of taking a step today, so that tomorrow you can reach your destination. Instead, celebrate the fact that you took a step today, and then use that celebration to stoke your drive and commitment to take the next up.

Finally, I want to remind you that risk is an inevitable part of anything that is worthwhile in this life. If you are afraid to take any risks at all you will never go anywhere. While it is prudent to minimize your risk wherever you can, at the same time you cannot allow your fear of taking a risk to hold you back and prevent you from even trying. The key is to find the acceptable balance of risk versus potential reward and then forge ahead while maintaining that balance, regardless of your fear. I knew a drill sergeant in the U.S. Army once, and he told me something that echoed within my being: "Great people are not those who have no fear; great people are those who acknowledge their fear and then act in spite of it."

If you keep these four things in mind and act accordingly I believe that there is nothing you cannot accomplish once you set your will to do so. So get out there, accept that you cannot truly fail, grit up, enjoy the small steps along the way, and act in spite of the risk. You are going to do great things.

Chapter 2

FEBRUARY: OVERESTIMATING THE IMPORTANCE OF INTELLIGENCE

Question: I know that everybody has problems and nobody is perfect. Yet, when I see other people who have achieved so much more than I have, I frequently feel like there's not much point in trying to amount to anything in life. I look at myself and I see someone who simply isn't very intelligent or talented, and I feel like I'm just not cut out for success. I have too many shortcomings and—quite frankly—I struggle with self-loathing. I'm not really sure where to go from here.

The first thing I would like to tell you is that I think you are overestimating the importance of intelligence and talent. While these two things are definitely helpful, they are not in and of themselves a requirement for success. The one requirement in order to succeed is perseverance and grit.

Secondly, regarding your feeling that you are simply not destined to be successful, I would encourage you to keep charging ahead and realize that success is a function of your determination to keep trying in spite of repeated failure. You are destined to succeed if you are willing to keep trying; in short, you determine your own destiny by how many times you are willing to pick yourself up and keep going.

Finally, while it is common to be somewhat disappointed after you have experienced what you believe to be a failure, I do not think that you should engage in self-loathing or self-recrimination. Regardless of what you may think or what you may feel the fact is that you are an amazing piece of work, so much so that the Creator only made one of you! Think about that for a moment: out of the more than seven billion people on this planet, there is no one else who is exactly like you and who has your exact mix of strengths and positive qualities!

> "It's not that I'm so smart, it's just that I stay with problems longer."
> — Albert Einstein

> "Let me tell you the secret that has led to my goal. My strength lies solely in my tenacity."
> — Louis Pasteur

First, I want to talk about this idea that you're not smart enough or talented enough to be a success. You need to realize that success is not a measure of how talented you are; nor is it a measure of how smart you are. Likewise, it is not a measure of how lucky you may be—although a little bit of luck certainly never hurts. On the contrary, whether you will succeed or not depends solely on one attribute, and the degree to which you possess this attribute is something that you can resolve to change if you wish to do so. That one attribute is your grit.

As we discussed in the last chapter grit is that quality that pushes you to get up no matter what is happening. Grit—or perseverance—is the only ingredient necessary to be a success. To be sure, if you are more talented than others or more intelligent than others—and especially if you are luckier than others—then, all else being equal, you will likely experience success faster than if you had no talent, intelligence, or luck. However, talent, intelligence, *and luck are completely irrelevant to the equation if you do not have grit.* Likewise, *if you have enough grit it will be sufficient to overcome a shortcoming of talent, intelligence, or luck.*

> *"A river cuts through rock, not because of its power, but because of its persistence."*
>
> — Jim Watkins

To put it differently, the only requirement is grit; other things may hasten the process but these other things by themselves are simply not sufficient to get the job done. Likewise, if you have the other things but lack grit, then you will never become the success you would like to be.

Let's use the analogy of a car. And for purposes of this illustration, we will greatly simplify the workings of a car. Let's say that four things are necessary for a car to move: an engine, tires, a steering wheel, and gasoline. Let's say that an engine is like intelligence: everyone has at least a small engine, while a select few have a larger engine. Tires are like ability: everyone has at least some, but some people have more ability (better tires). A steering wheel is like luck: it helps to have a bigger wheel (more luck) but everyone is capable of at least developing something that will get the job done (generally speaking, luck is the result of hard work and planning).

So, to what do we liken your grit; your tenacity? That is the gasoline. Think about it: you can have a nice car with a big engine, great tires, and a high-performance steering wheel, but if you only have a few cups of gasoline in the tank, that car is not going to go very far.

On the other hand, even if you have a small engine, worn tires, and a rickety little steering wheel, if you have a limitless supply of gasoline you can go as far as you want to go. It might take you longer to get there than it would if you had all of the other things, but you will get there nonetheless.

The length to which you can go is not a function of the size of your engine, the quality of your tires, or the width of your steering wheel. Rather, the length to which you can go is directly related to the amount of gasoline (or grit) you possess. The world's biggest engine, nicest tires, and the most expensive steering wheel won't do you a bit of good if you have no gas to put in the tank.

So, keeping in mind the analogy of a car, which would you rather possess: talent, intelligence, luck, or perseverance? I think the answer is clear: the first three items will certainly help you, but are inadequate to get you to your destination, unless you have an adequate supply of the last item.

I do not dispute that some people are more intelligent and more talented than others. Nor do I dispute the usefulness of these qualities. However, these qualities are not required for you to arrive at your destination of success. *In order to reach your goal, the only thing that is <u>absolutely required</u> is an adequate supply of grit.* And, as I mentioned earlier, you can make the determination within yourself to increase your grit. Intelligence and talent are things which are given to you and, while they can be developed, you cannot will yourself to have more of them; on the other hand, the amount of grit you possess is directly related to your desire to continue persevering no matter what happens.

So, instead of being concerned that you may not possess enough intelligence or talent, you need to reach deep within yourself and stoke the fires of your resolve. Make the determination right now that <u>no matter what, you</u> will not quit trying until you have reached your goals. That determination—that resolution—is well and truly the only thing that actually matters.

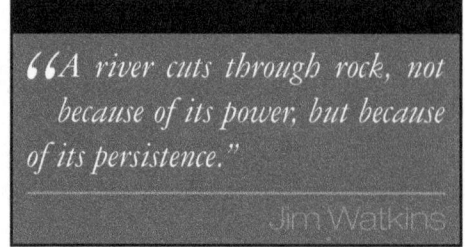

"*A river cuts through rock, not because of its power, but because of its persistence.*"

Jim Watkins

Next I want to address your idea that perhaps you are not 'cut out' to be a success. I want to share a secret with you and that secret is this: because the accomplishment of your goals depends entirely upon your own perseverance and grit, you actually control your own destiny in the matter of whether you will be a success or not.

The idea that some people are simply not meant to succeed is a falsehood invented by people who no longer have the desire to keep going. Because they want to quit, they begin to invent reasons why it would be okay to quit. Think about it: it is a lot easier to justify giving up when you have convinced yourself that giving up is perfectly acceptable because you will not be a success regardless.

If you choose to give up that is your right to do so, but I want you to be very clear about one thing: you are giving up because you do not wish to keep trying, not because it does not matter what you do. On the contrary, it matters very much what you do.

History is full of illustrations of tenacity and the results therefrom. I said it earlier and I will say it again: you have the ability to determine your own destiny by determining whether you will continue to try or whether you will quit. So you cannot—indeed you *must not*—lie to yourself and convince yourself that it doesn't matter what you do anyway. The idea that you're fated to fail regardless is a lie that quitters tell themselves because they *want* to quit.

But you are not a quitter. I can tell that because you wrote me asking this question. That tells me that deep within you there does burn the desire to achieve great things. So I want to encourage you to feed the flames of passion and determine right now—once for all—that you will keep going no matter how many times you fall down. Keep going, and eventually you will reach your goal. Then you will look back on your journey with a

> "Love yourself first and everything else falls into line. You really have to love yourself to get anything done in this world."
>
> Lucille Ball

certain amount of fondness and proclaim, "I did it! I knew I could do it and I never gave up!"

> **If you can't believe in miracles, then believe in yourself. When you want something bad enough, let that drive push you to make it happen. Sometimes you'll run into brick walls that are put there to test you. Find a way around them and stay focused on your dream. Where there's a will, there's a way."**
>
> Isabel Lopez, *Isabel's Hand-Me-Down Dreams*

Finally, I want to talk with you about your feelings of self-loathing. Understand your position in the universe: there is only one of you and you are incredibly capable and wonderfully made. Out of all the people that have ever existed on this planet, nobody has been exactly like you. Nobody has had the exact same capabilities that you have. You are unique!

Because you are unique you must realize how valuable you are. You are very precious to the Creator and to those around you. Nobody else can ever take your place. Nobody else can ever do exactly the same things that you do exactly the way that you do them. You are a walking, talking miracle!

In my experience, feelings of self-loathing often come about because we are disappointed in something that has happened. However, from here on out you never again need to be disappointed in anything because, as we discovered in the last chapter, you will never truly fail. Because you'll never fail you never have any reason to be disappointed. Instead, you can treat each situation—whether it is something you planned on or not—as a part of your progress towards success.

Love yourself because you are special. Believe in yourself because there is no one else out there exactly like you. And acknowledge that your feeling of self-loathing really is simply disappointment in disguise and—because you now are aware of the fact that you will never fail again—there will never again be a need to be disappointed.

Conclusion

While talent and skill are helpful in your path towards success they are certainly not crucial. Rather, the one thing that is crucial—your grit and perseverance—is one thing that you can actually control how much of it you possess. Because of this you should be thankful for what talent and skill you have but you should not feel defeated simply because you may not possess as much as you think other people do. At the end of the day what will determine whether you are a success or not is the amount of grit in your tank and, fortunately, you have the ability to will yourself to have as much grit as you want to have.

The idea that you are simply not fated to be a success is a lie that you tell yourself when you want to justify giving up. In truth, we all make our own destiny, and so long as you continue to grit up and keep working to achieve your goal you will find that you are actually fated to succeed.

Finally, of the more than seven billion people on the planet today, there is nobody else exactly like you. You should realize just how important you are to the Creator and to the grand scheme of things. Instead of allowing disappointment to come to you and take the guise of self-loathing, you should instead celebrate the fact that you will never again fail at anything to which you truly set your mind to. Because you'll never again fail, you will never again feel disappointment, and you can celebrate the fact that you are a wonderful and unique—and yes even a very *valuable*—miracle.

CHAPTER 3

MARCH: YOU ARE NOT A QUITTER!

Question: When I was younger, I tried to reach a personal goal of mine. I did not make it and, although I would say I definitely learned something from the experience, I also have some scars from it. You see, during the course of the events that ultimately led to me not reaching my goal, I said some things of which I am very ashamed to some people. I have apologized, and it seems that everyone has forgiven me and moved on, but I am still haunted both by the fact that I did not achieve my goal and by the things I said.

start, I would like to say that I'm very encouraged by your question because it shows me that you are already on the right track. For one thing, you acknowledge that you learned something from your experience. For another, you have already done what is in your power to make things right with the people that you feel you wronged; this tells me that you have already started down the right path towards moving on with your life and reaching your goals. Because you have such a good start, I think that you are much closer to achieving greatness than you may realize.

I would like to start off by focusing on the matter of what you perceived as a failure to reach your personal goal. As we discussed in chapter one you never truly fail so long as you put everything you have into reaching your goal, and you take away something from the experience.

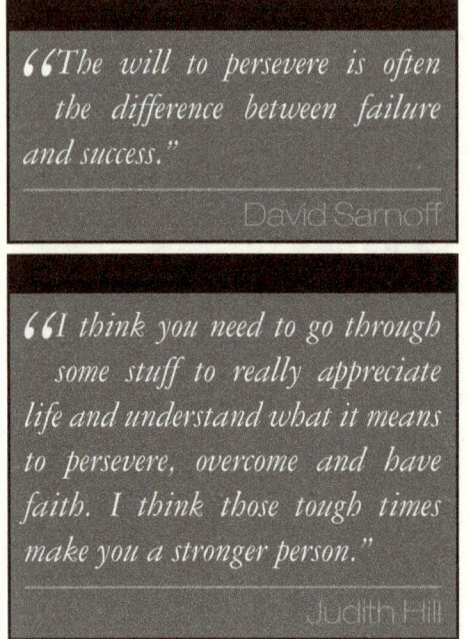

> "The will to persevere is often the difference between failure and success."
> — David Sarnoff

> "I think you need to go through some stuff to really appreciate life and understand what it means to persevere, overcome and have faith. I think those tough times make you a stronger person."
> — Judith Hill

Even though you may not have reached the outcome for which you were aiming, the fact of the matter is the experience was a success: like you, yourself noted, you learned something from the experience. Thus, the entire experience was simply one step in the process towards reaching your ultimate goal.

I would like to encourage you to go back and reread my discussion on what a failure is—and what a failure is not—in chapter one. Once we have established that your experience was truly, not a failure, then we should turn our eye towards considering where you should go from here.

I selected the above quotes because I think they underscore the importance of perseverance. Perseverance is one thing you must have if you are ever to reach your goals. I sincerely doubt that anyone has ever made a noteworthy discovery or reached a meaningful goal without experiencing at least some adversity along the way.

Because adversity is pretty much a given along the path towards greatness—actually, I will go ahead and say that adversity, absolutely is a given along this path—that quality that you must display is your tenacity and grit.

You already have a great start on the road to greatness because you have already evaluated the situation and determined what you learned the first time around. Now, what you must do next is to take what you learned and apply it during your next attempt.

At the same time, you must resolve within yourself that you will not quit, no matter what happens. Sometimes people read what I have to say about showing grit and they are inspired to rise up and try again (which is good) but then when they hit their next patch of adversity (which is a given, remember) they become discouraged all over again and decide that all this talk about perseverance is just a bunch of nonsense.

You have to keep in mind that the path to greatness will take you through many different types of adversity. You cannot have it in your head that you simply need to rise up one time and then everything will be roses. On the contrary, you need to be clear that you will stumble and fall again and again and again. What will make you great during this time is the perseverance to grit up and keep going *no matter how many times it takes.*

I would say that you have not failed in this matter; rather, as Thomas Jefferson stated, you simply discovered one way that did not work. Now it is time for you to take what you learned and apply it towards your next endeavor. At the same time, you must be fully prepared for the high likelihood that your next attempt will also end with results other than what you are expecting, and that's OK: remember, every attempt is simply a step in the process and—after you take enough steps—you will eventually reach your goal.

Now I would like to discuss the matter of your regret over the things that you said to some people in your life. I selected these quotes because they show that you can still be great while

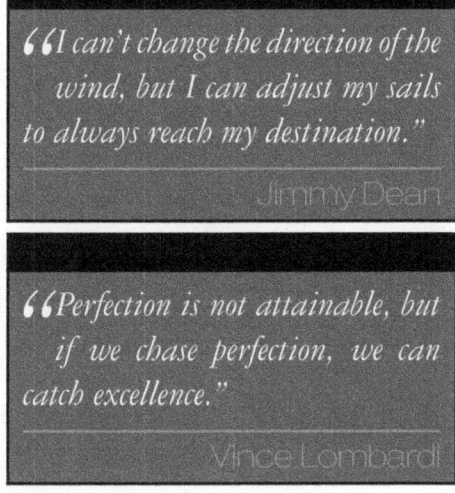

" I can't change the direction of the wind, but I can adjust my sails to always reach my destination."

Jimmy Dean

"Perfection is not attainable, but if we chase perfection, we can catch excellence."

Vince Lombardi

at the same time acknowledging that, first, you are not perfect and, second, there are some things that you simply cannot change—namely, what has happened in the past.

I would like to begin this portion of our discussion by pointing out something that you probably believe to be so obvious that it does not need to be stated: nobody is perfect. That's right, every single person on this planet has made and will continue to make mistakes that he or she probably would rather not make.

In spite of the self-evident nature of this declaration I believe it bears repeating because many times we forget this fact and expect perfection either from others or—more commonly—from ourselves. Remember that everyone makes mistakes and you are part of *everyone*. This means that you will make mistakes.

Accepting that you will make mistakes, the question then becomes what you can and should do when a mistake occurs. I would submit that you approach it exactly the same way that you approach a situation where you attempt to reach a goal, and you obtain an outcome other than the one you expected. This is to say, although you may make a mistake you will never truly have a failure so long as you give everything you have, and you learn something from the situation.

For example, I would guess that you probably learned something from the situation where you said something that you now regret. Perhaps you have learned that when you start to feel stressed it is a good idea to give yourself a time out and go for a walk before you make any phone calls. Or, perhaps you learned that you can only handle so much at one time without losing your cool and saying something that you will later regret.

In either case, this is something that you have learned and something that you can apply to your life from here on out. As such, although you said something that you wish you could take back, the fact of the matter is that you learned from the situation, and you are now a better person because of it. As such, although you may wish that you had not said the things that you did because you took something out of the situation that you may apply in your life going forward, I would not consider this to be a mistake or a failure.

On the one hand, it is good that you expect so much from yourself. To expect perfection from yourself shows that you are not satisfied with anything other than success. On the other hand, remember that nobody is perfect, and that includes you. So don't be so hard on yourself; rather, treat it as a learning experience and take something out of it that you may apply to your life going forward.

Finally, if it makes you feel better, I would point out that you, yourself stated that the people you wronged have forgiven you. If they have forgiven you then perhaps it is time you realize that you need to forgive yourself. We are frequently our own worst critic and nowhere is this statement truer than in the realm of personal regrets that we may have about things we have said.

> *"The rewards for those who persevere far exceed the pain that must precede the victory."*
> — Ted Engstrom

So, because others have forgiven you, you need to forgive yourself and move on. This is where you show your grit: you must pick yourself up off the ground, dust yourself off, and get back to work.

In light of what I've shared here about applying what you have learned and accepting your imperfections while at the same time determining to continue towards your goal, I just have one thing left to say: grit up and keep going.

You have a prime opportunity here to show what you are made of. Adversity does not just test your character; also, I would say that adversity actually reveals what type of character you have. Here you are in a situation where you have been disappointed, both by the results of your previous endeavor as well as by the things that you said during the experience. So what will you do now? Will you lay down and quit? Or will you pick yourself up and keep moving?

> *"The most inspiring piece of advice I've gotten is simply to persevere. My mom taught me to always keep going no matter what from an early age. When it feels too difficult to push forward, I always remind myself, 'This too shall pass,' and then I redouble my efforts."*
>
> — Liya Kebede

As tough as things might seem at the present time, remember that at some point—when you stand at the pinnacle of your accomplishment and look back over the path that you took to get there—the way that you feel right now will simply be a memory. Indeed, I would say that the very fact that you are going through some adversity will make the eventual triumph that much sweeter.

However, you will never get there unless you grit up and get going. You must determine deep within your being that you will not quit; in fact, you should determine that every time you encounter adversities they will only act to deepen your resolve and spur you ever onward to greater things.

Conclusion

Remember that achieving an outcome other than the one you were expecting is not a failure so long as you gave it your best shot and you learned something from the experience. Because you have already said that you did learn something, I think you are in a great position to take your next step towards success.

Also, remember that nobody is perfect—, and this includes you. When you say or do something that you wish you had not said or done you should approach it the same way that you approach the situation when you achieve an outcome besides the one you expected. This is to say, assuming that you really did give it your best shot, you need to treat it as a learning experience and move on with your life. Everybody says things that he or she wish they had not said; you cannot turn back the clock, so the best thing you can do is take something out of the experience and apply it to your life going forward.

Finally, you have to determine within yourself that you are going to keep striving no matter what. You cannot quit every time you run into trouble. You cannot quit every time you say something you wish you had not said. Rather, you must pick yourself up, roll up your sleeves, and jump right back into the fray one more time.

In closing, I would like to remind you of the famous scene in Shakespeare's classic *Henry the Fifth*. King Henry V is giving a speech to rally his army to join the battle yet one more time and keep fighting no matter what. I think it is very fitting in your case because, although you have undoubtedly suffered some adversity, what you need to do now is turn back once more and get back to business.

> Once more unto the breach, dear friends, once more;
> Or close the wall up with our . . . dead. . . .
>
> But when the blast of war blows in our ears,
> Then imitate the action of the tiger. . . .[1]

---

1 Shakespeare, William. *Henry the Fifth, Act 3, scene 1,* 1–6

CHAPTER 4

APRIL: THE NEW LEAF AND THE CREATOR

Question: I was raised in a home with a strong faith. As I became an adult and began to step out into the world, I was severely disappointed in some of the experiences I had. Namely, it seemed that everything I put my hand to turned out to be a failure. These series of events ended up costing me my belief in my own abilities as well as my belief in God. I felt—and to some extent still feel—that if God were real, He would not let my life be such a colossal failure.

I think you need to keep a few things in mind. First, the fact that it seemed "everything [you] put your hand to turned out to be a failure" actually tells me some good things about you (more on that in a moment). Second, I think you need to reassess your loss of faith and remember some key points about the Creator.

I chose the above quote because it brings out the importance of turning over a new leaf regardless of what has happened before. I am going to spend some time discussing what you perceive to be failures and then I am going to encourage you to start anew.

> "The chief beauty about time is that you cannot waste it in advance. The next year, the next day, the next hour are lying ready for you, as perfect, as unspoiled, as if you had never wasted or misapplied a single moment in all your life. You can turn over a new leaf every hour if you choose."
>
> Arnold Bennett

You seem to think that you are something of a failure because so many of your endeavors ended in a way other than what you had anticipated and hoped. However, this tells me something very important about you: you are not satisfied with mediocrity. How do I know this? Simple. If you were one of those people who is easily satisfied with a mediocre outcome, then you would never have undertaken any type of endeavor that posed a challenge.

Let me put that differently: the fact that your efforts brought in results other than the ones you were expecting tells me that you must have been endeavoring to achieve something at least moderately challenging. If you were only aiming for mediocrity, then your attempts would have surely succeeded because mediocrity is something that is easily attainable. Excellence, on the other hand, requires a great deal of effort, and the fact that you did not reach your goals tells me that you were aiming high, and that's *a good thing!*

So, having established that you have set your goals at a high level, what should your next step be in light of your earlier experiences? Well, if you take a look back at chapter one and even—to a lesser extent—chapter three of this book, you will see that I encourage people to reassess what they consider to be a *failure*.

Did you learn anything from your previous experiences that could help you the next time you reach for your goals? If yes, then I certainly would not consider them to be a failure. If not, I actually still would not consider them to be a failure because if nothing else they helped me to assess the type of person you are so that I can give you the advice I will be dispensing in the rest of this chapter. As such, no matter which way you look at it, I would not consider your previous experiences to be failures.

Because you are clearly someone with high goals I want to encourage you to reach for them again. I want you to take some time and think over what you would like to do with your life. Then I would like for you to come up with a way to bridge the gap between where you are right now and where you would like to be in the long-term.

But as readers of my previous book will tell you simply having a plan to get from here to there is not by itself going to be sufficient. I tell you this because one thing is certain: you will experience many roadblocks and, when you do, you must have the grit to overcome adversity.

You must develop a tenacity to continue striving for your goals regardless of how many times it seems to you that you have run into a wall. The number one requirement for reaching your goals is perseverance. Without perseverance, you will simply not make it because—as you have already shown me by your question—you have a desire for excellence, and excellence does not come without gritting up and continuing on through many challenges.

I want to spend some time encouraging you to brush yourself off and start anew in spite of what may have happened in your past. You are not able to turn back the clock

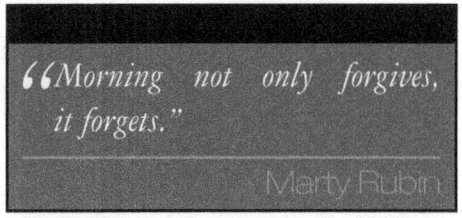

"Morning not only forgives, it forgets."
—Marty Rubin

and change what has happened. While at first this might sound a little bit discouraging, the fact is it is actually very liberating: it means that you do not have to spend time wallowing in self regret or playing the "What if?" game because you know that no matter how much time you spend doing these things, the past is the past, and it will forever remain unchanged.

Because you cannot change what happened in the past you should use that to motivate you so that 20 years from today, you are not sitting around regretting what you did at this point in your life. You cannot change the past, but you can certainly act now so that tomorrow you do not have any regrets about today.

In a very real sense today is the *morning* for the rest of your life. It is the new beginning from which you will spring to greater and higher accomplishments than you ever thought possible. Instead of wasting time regretting what happened *last night* you should instead seize the *morning* you have right now and began living the rest of your life the way that you want to live it.

Life is too short to spend it shackled by self-regret and vain wishes about changing yesterday. Because you know that yesterday is already passed and there is nothing you can do to change it, you need to make peace with that fact and prepare to move on with the rest of your life.

You have a new beginning today. Now it is up to you how you will proceed with the rest of your life. Will you act now so that in 20 years you look back and consider how wonderful the journey has been? Or, will you waste more time today wallowing in sorrow about yesterday, so that nothing changes in your life between now and then? The choice is up to you.

> *"And we know that all things work together for good to those who love God, who have been called according to his purpose."*
> Romans 8:28

Now I want to spend some time talking with you about the loss of your faith and your inability to apprehend why the Creator would allow some of the things that have happened to occur in your life. I chose the above quotes because it is a classic verse out of the Bible showing how the Creator works in the lives of those whom he has called.

Frequently when we encounter difficulties in life we begin to wonder what the purpose of it all is. It is easy to get discouraged—especially because we do not see the big picture—and feel like things are pointless or, worse yet, that the Creator has some grand purpose to ruin us.

Actually, nothing could be further from the truth! Remember that the Creator loves you very much and he has a wonderful plan for your life. To this end, you must also remember that everything that happens to you will eventually work out for good.

Let me use a rather simple analogy here to illustrate the relationship that we have with the Creator and some of the things that he does to take care of us. If you have ever given birth to a child you know that one of the first things we do in the first several months of life is to give the child a number of different shots and inoculations in order to help the child ward off disease and illness throughout his or her life.

Now, when that child is getting a shot, it is a rather painful experience. What's worse, because he or she does not have the capacity to see into the future like we do, it seems to be a rather pointless experience. All the child knows is that he or she is in pain and it seems like there is no point to it.

But nothing could be further from the truth! There is very much a point of giving the shots: the vaccinations allow the child to live a normal, healthy life and to be free to run and play outside without fear of catching some terrible illness.

Consider that the Creator is the father of us all. What's more, he sees much further down the road than we do. He knows what is coming and he knows what we need to go through right now in order to prepare us for what we will face later on.

Sometimes we may experience things in life that we genuinely consider to be a suffering. Just like the baby suffers when he or she is receiving a vaccination, we may truly suffer when we are going through an experience in life. However, this does not mean that there is no point to the suffering. On the contrary, the point is that by suffering a little bit right now we can be saved from much greater suffering later on down the road.

Sometimes when we do not understand what is happening it is simply enough to know that the Creator cares about us and He has us in His hand. He knows exactly what He is doing and we may rest in that knowledge. We may not understand much about tomorrow, but we don't *need* to because we understand who it is that holds tomorrow—and us—in His hand.

I think that if you consider your past experiences in this light it will help you to see that the Creator was preparing you, even then, for some things that will come later on. There is a classic poem entitled *Footprints in the Sand*. For the sake of space, I will not reproduce the entire thing here.

Briefly, the poem tells a story of someone who was walking along the beach with the Creator. Looking back the person sees that the tracks represent various stages of life. Further, the person notices that during the particularly dark and stormy periods of life there was only one set of footprints. The person turns and asks the Creator about this, believing that the one set of footprints showed that God had left during those periods. The Creator's response was that, on the contrary, the times when there was only one set of prints were actually times where he had carried the person.

I believe this poem aptly describes our experiences in life. With this in mind, I would like to encourage you to turn again to your faith and thank your Creator for his faithfulness. He never leaves us, nor does he forsake us. He is always there, carrying us through the storms.

Conclusion

The fact that you did not easily accomplish your goals earlier in life tells me that you have high standards. Rather than viewing your experiences as failures, you can instead view them as a step in the process of reaching your goals. I want to encourage you to start again and focus on your goal; never wavering and never backing down until you get there.

Today is a new start for you. Regardless of what has happened up until this point in your life, today you are able to start anew and write the story of the rest of your life. Don't waste time bemoaning what happened yesterday or sitting around wishing you could go back and change the past. You cannot; so put it to bed and move on. Make peace with your past and move on to tomorrow.

Finally, remember that your Creator has nothing but good in his heart for you. Although you may not understand everything that happens, you may rest in the knowledge that he arranges everything for your own good and one day you will look back and be amazed at how perfectly he did everything. He loves you and he is faithfully working in your life—often behind the scenes—to bring you to the destiny which he has set aside for you.

CHAPTER 5

MAY: BELIEVE...
YOU HAVE
WHAT IT TAKES

Question: I have some things that I would like to do in my life, but from where I am standing it seems that achieving my goals is an impossibility. Due to some factors outside of my control I am at a disadvantage when it comes to reaching my goals. Although I think that someone else—perhaps someone born into a better position than I, or born with some different abilities than mine—could achieve my goals, I'm just not sure that I personally can do it. What advice do you have for someone who believes that they simply cannot reach their goals?

There are two things that I would say to you. First, I need to encourage you to believe in yourself. You must believe that you possess every attribute which is necessary to accomplish your goals. If you do not believe in yourself, then you will never take the steps which are necessary to reach your desired outcome.

Second, you must believe that you are every bit as capable of reaching your goals as every other person on the planet. Yes, perhaps the position into which others were born or some of the abilities that you may not have would assist in reaching your goals, but these things are by no means *necessary* to get to your destination; there is a significant difference between *helpful and necessary.* The only thing that is necessary is the desire to get there and the determination that you will not give up.

> *"If you hear a voice within you say 'you cannot paint,' then by all means paint, and that voice will be silenced."*
> — Vincent van Gogh

I want to start out by talking about the necessity of believing in yourself. If you do not believe in yourself then you are defeated before you start because you will never bother to take the first step on your journey towards success. If you truly believe that you cannot do something you will not bother trying to do it and so, you'll never see that you actually can do it.

You spend some time mentioning the things that you do not have, such as certain skills and attributes or even a certain position in life. However, what I never saw you talk about was all the things that you do have. Think about that for a moment. You possess a great number of things which can be valuable to you on your journey to success.

Even the fact that you bothered to contact me shows a positive attribute on your part: you are wise enough to determine when you need assistance, and you are humble enough to accept that assistance. Now think about the other attributes that you possess. Surely you

> *"Don't wait until everything is just right. It will never be perfect. There will always be challenges, obstacles, and less than perfect conditions. So what? Get started now. With each step you take, you will grow stronger and stronger, more and more skilled, more and more self-confident, and more and more successful."*
> — Mark Victor Hansen

have a number of things that will help you reach your goals. Maybe you do not have as much of a certain attribute as you would like to have, but certainly you possess enough of it that—with a sufficient amount of grit and determination—you can certainly reach your goals.

Let me use an illustration. Let us say that your goal is to chop down a certain large tree in the woods behind your house. Likewise, your next door neighbor also would like to chop down the tree. Now let us suppose that you only own a small hand axe, while your neighbor owns an expensive chainsaw.

Who do you think will be able to chop down the tree? The answer is this: the person who really wants to do it. Your neighbor might be able to cut through wood faster than you can but if he only cuts for a few minutes and then gets tired and gives up that tree will remain standing. Likewise, although it might take you longer to cut through the same amount of wood, if you keep at it long enough, then you can take down that tree even though you are only using a small hand axe.

In this illustration the cutting tools owned by you and your neighbor are analogous to your respective abilities. Perhaps someone else has greater ability than you do. However, keep in mind that no matter how small you might feel your ability to be, in the end it will be sufficient to get the job done as long as you are willing to keep working until you get there.

So, coming back to the matter of what you believe about yourself, I think you are not being fair to yourself in saying that you are not able to reach your goal. A more accurate statement would be, "I cannot progress towards my goal as quickly as I could if I had a greater measure of ability, but I definitely can make progress nonetheless, and I will continue to proceed towards my goal without giving up until I get there."

Do you see the distinction? I am not disputing that other people might seem to be better equipped or to possess certain advantages that you may not possess; what I am saying is that someone else's abilities or any advantages they may have is *completely irrelevant to the question of whether you can reach your goal.*

Don't spend so much time comparing yourself to other people. Instead, take stock of the abilities that you do possess and the tools that you have in your "tool chest" and make the determination that you are going to keep working no matter what until you get to your goal. At the end of the day, it is not the size of the "axe" that you are using to cut the tree so much as it is the number of times you are willing to swing it.

> *"You may encounter many defeats, but you must not be defeated. In fact, it may be necessary to encounter the defeats, so you can know who you are, what you can rise from, how you can still come out of it."*
> — Maya Angelou

I would like to spend a few moments to encourage you to pick yourself up in spite of any adversity you may have experienced in the past. When you set your sights on a goal and then you run into a roadblock in the way, that roadblock should not serve to deter you; rather, it should actually encourage you to keep going because you know that when you finally reach your goal it will be that much sweeter due to the difficulties you had to overcome along the way.

If you always achieved everything that you set your mind to on the first attempt, you would never have any opportunity to build your character. Character is not built by repeated successes; rather, character is the thing which is developed through repeated encounters with adversity and the steps which you take to overcome.

You must resolve deep within your being that you will not give up regardless of how many times you encounter adversity. Instead, you must pick yourself up again, and again, and again and hurl yourself once more at the object which hinders you from continuing on.

If you have ever seen the Grand Canyon you know what a marvelous sight it is. The pictures that you may have seen simply do not do it justice. Stretching out over miles and miles in reaching deep into the earth, it is truly a magnificent sight.

Now, do you know how it was formed? It was formed by water flowing across the surface year after year after year. Each year that the water flowed it carried a tiny amount of the earth and rock away with it. Over the span of 17 million years the water continually flowed, never stopping, never quitting, and always making progress.

If you were around during the formation of the Grand Canyon, you may have crouched down over one of the streams and thought to yourself "Nothing is happening. This is no deeper than it was last year, or the year before that." But you would have been wrong. Something was happening, albeit at an extremely slow pace.

You need to determine that you are going to be like the water flowing across the rock. This means that you must determine that you will continue working even when it seems like nothing is happening. Even if you do not feel like you're making progress you must not give up. Instead, you should put your head down and redouble your efforts.

As you continue working towards your goal, you will eventually notice that bit by bit you are getting closer. And that is all that you need to know: in spite of the difficulty, in spite of the seeming pointlessness of your continued endeavors, *you are making progress.*

> *Should you shield the canyons from the windstorms, you would never see the true beauty of their carvings.*
>
> Elisabeth Kübler-Ross

Having grit is having the determination that you will not quit even when you have been "flowing" over the "rock" for years and years without making much progress. What would have happened if the water flowing through the Grand Canyon had one day decided to quit because it wasn't making any progress? Aside from the obvious silliness of the question because water does not think, the answer is: nothing. That's right, nothing would have happened. And instead of the beautiful, majestic national treasure that we have today we would just have some rock out in the middle of the desert.

You need to have the grit to keep working even when it feels like nothing is happening. Keep going towards your goal no matter how many times it seems that you have fallen down. You can never give up; you must pick yourself up again and again and get back to work.

Conclusion

We have talked about how necessary it is for you to believe in yourself. If you do not believe in yourself, then you will never take the first step on your journey to success. You must believe that you are capable of reaching your goals. I know that you are capable because you had the inner fire which caused you to reach out to me for help; this shows me that you do have a drive to succeed and—although the path may be long and arduous—you have every tool that you need to reach your goal.

In addition, remember that there is a difference between an advantage and a requirement when it comes to reaching your goals. Having more of a certain attribute than you do might be an advantage but it is certainly not a requirement. The only thing that is required for you to reach your goal is tenacity and grit. Remember the illustration of using a chainsaw or a hand axe to cut down the tree: the person who will cut the tree down is the person who wants it badly enough.

Finally, remember that you have to have the inner determination to keep working towards your goals regardless of what happens. The Grand Canyon was not formed in a day; likewise, you will most certainly not attain your lofty ambitions in just a few short years. Just as the water continued to flow year after year, century after century, inevitably wearing away the rock a little bit at a time, so too you must continue working steadfastly towards your goal. It may take you a long time to reach it—and it will almost certainly be accomplished one small step at a time—but you *will* get there.

I believe in you, and now you must believe in yourself. All it takes is grit and determination to get there.

CHAPTER 6

JUNE: GROW UP

Question: I have just crossed into middle age in my life and I have achieved a fair amount of success. Although I am not quite where I always have hoped I would be, at the same time I cannot dispute that I have at least moderately succeeded in life. Should I be content in the knowledge that at least I have not failed, or should it bother me that I never achieved my highest goals?

First, I would like to congratulate you on the modest amount of success that you have enjoyed. It is always good to be thankful for the small things and that absolutely includes the successes and accomplishments that we have enjoyed along the journey of life.

Now, in response to your question, I want to tell you that I'm very encouraged that you see things quite clearly. This is to say you understand that—while you have accomplished some things—you know that things could be better. It is good that you can see this because it will save you from resting on your laurels and becoming complacent.

I want to encourage you to hold yourself to the highest standard. Don't ever expect or accept anything less than the very best from yourself. By holding yourself to a higher standard and always "staying hungry" you will be forced to continue growing as a person where you otherwise may have stopped. The day that you turn and say "I've made it!" is the day that you stop growing.

> *"The problem with thinking that you are the absolute best, is that it leaves no room for you to become any better and while you live life thinking that you're the best, truth is a lot of people around you are already better and becoming even more better."*
> — C. Joy Bell C.

I want to start our discussion by encouraging you to never believe that there is no room for improvement. From your question it sounds like you are aware of the fact that you could have done better (even if you have done moderately well). This is a good thing to keep in mind because this way you leave yourself room to grow.

One of the strongest motivators that people have is the desire to be the best that they can be. It is one thing to compete against other people; it is something else entirely to compete against yourself. When you are competing against other people it is sufficient simply to be better than the others, however, this approach will not bring out the very best in you. At most it will bring out just enough to beat everyone else in the room.

On the other hand, when you are not satisfied with where you are simply because you know that there is room to grow—regardless of where you might stand in relation to other people—then you will never quit; you will never stop; you will never give up; you will never stop striving to be better until you have reached that place where you know deep within your being that you are the best that you possibly can be.

Now that I have encouraged you to continue striving until you are the best that you possibly can be I want to encourage you to likewise *never accept the proposition that you are as good as you can be.* For one thing, we never stopped growing, so this is simply a fallacy. For another thing, to accept this idea is to likewise accept that it's OK for you to stop trying to improve yourself. You never want to put yourself in this position.

I am glad that you admit that things could have gone better with your life. Admitting this fact will save you from becoming complacent. It will save you from thinking that you have already arrived and there is no need to keep trying.

At the same time, I want to encourage you to believe that you have not yet reached your ceiling. It is good that you have enjoyed a modest amount of success, but there is so much more that you can do. You need to resolve deep within your being that you will not settle for "better than a failure" or "kind of a success" but instead you will drive yourself to continue fighting and continue working until you have reached the highest goals that you set for yourself. And then—once you reach your goal—you can set new ones to spur yourself on to ever higher levels of excellence.

You must never stop growing, you must never stop striving. You have to remain hungry for success no matter how much you might want to believe that you have already reached the peak of your ability. The fact of the matter is—no matter how high you have gone—you can always go higher, and you should be satisfied with nothing less than the highest accomplishments out of yourself.

> *People usually live up to their expectations. The kid picked first for Dodgeball feels a duty to be the best, and to perform the best, and to be better than anyone else. They feel a need to execute. And, the only way they are going to achieve that is to make their body run faster, jump higher, and move quicker.*

> *If more fat kids were chosen first for activities and sports and group/team dynamics, they would automatically start to change their lives to fit into the expectations that surround those moments. Any time a child is picked last, they know it's because people expect the least of them, and so they never actually have a need to rise above that.*"

Dan Pearce, Single Dad Laughing

There is a reason that I encourage you to expect nothing less than the very best out of yourself. It is because there is a very basic principle when it comes to human behavior, and that principle is this: you will always tend towards what is expected of you. If you are expected to reach only a mediocre level of success in life you, will find yourself being irresistibly drawn to mediocrity; on the other hand, if you are expected to reach the highest levels of success and accomplishment, you will find that these very expectations, are the things which propel you on and push you to keep going even when you would otherwise like to lay down and quit.

The bad news is that the expectations placed on you will impact the level to which you rise; the good news is that the expectations placed on you will impact the level to which you rise! You see, you will not be bound or restricted by the expectations of other people; rather the expectations which will so strongly impact your level of excellence are your own expectations for yourself.

This means that you can actually affect your level of success by the expectations that you hold for yourself! If you expect that you will only be mediocre, then that is the level to which you will rise—and no higher. If you expect that you will be a miserable failure at everything you put your hand to, then you will discover yourself inexplicably failing again and again and again. At the same time, if you expect nothing less than the very best out of yourself, then you will find yourself continually reaching new heights and accomplishing greater things.

I frequently talk about the quality of grit that you have within your being. If you have a significant level of perseverance and determination such that you can resolve within yourself to keep pushing towards your goals regardless of what happens then you will find those goals to be attainable regardless of how difficult they might seem at the outset.

The reason I bring up grit in the context of your self-expectations is that the latter will actually have an effect on the former. If you have the expectation that you will be the very best at what you do, this expectation will fuel within you a fire that will continually burn, always pushing you to pick yourself up and keep trying. On the other hand, if you expect that mediocre is about the best that you can do, then you will discover that as you near mediocrity your desire and drive to continue excelling will begin to die out.

This is because deep within you there will be the reasoning which says, "I have already gone as high as I'm going to go. Since I cannot go any higher there is no point in trying anymore. I may as well just sit down and rest here and let others go on to higher in greater things." Whether you actually reason it out like this or not, that is the sentiment that will be echoing within your being.

Therefore, because grit is the one quality that is crucial to your success, I would say that the one *belief* that is crucial to your success is the belief that you can always be better and that you *will continue to get better and better* no matter how high you may have already risen.

In addition to determining within yourself that you will not quit—no matter what, no matter how many times you fall down—you also need to make the decision today that you will expect nothing less than the very best out of yourself while, at the same time, acknowledging that there's always room for improvement.

Conclusion

In a nutshell, it is good to realize that you can go higher than you have already gone while—at the same time—expecting nothing other than the very best out of yourself. Approaching your life with this mindset will both save you from becoming complacent and at the same time will push you on to continually achieve greater things because greater things is what you expect out of yourself.

If you think that you are the best already then you will leave yourself no room to grow. On the other hand, if you realize that you're not the best, but—at the same time—you believe that you're probably about as good as you are capable of getting, then you will have no motivation to grit up and keep trying when you run into adversities.

You have to set the highest standard for yourself and never rest until you reach that standard. Further, once you do reach one of the goals that you have set for yourself, the best way to approach it is to celebrate the accomplishments on the one hand while looking to set new (higher) goals for yourself on the other hand.

I know that you have the potential to be great. All you need to do is apply the principles that we have covered in the previous chapters as well as the things we will discuss in the rest of this book. Don't ever settle for anything but the best out of yourself; at the same time always be aware that you have more room to grow.

CHAPTER 7

JULY: FOLLOW YOUR HEART WITH PASSION

Question: What am I supposed to do when I reach a point where I am at a crossroads and I don't know which route to take? Also, what if I know the path I want to take but the task in front of me just seems too large to tackle?

Well, your question actually has two parts, with two distinct answers. First, when it comes to deciding which path to follow, then I want to urge you to follow your heart (assuming all other things are equal). Following your heart—as trite as it sounds—will give you the passion you need to keep going when you are tired and want to quit.

Regarding your second question, the way to tackle a large task is simply to take it one step at a time. A long journey is made up of many, many distinct steps. So too should your approach to a larger goal be divided up into many *sub-steps.*

When it comes to needing direction in your life, of course, you want to consider practical things such as the amount of time and effort it will take you to achieve your goals. If you are trying to decide between two alternatives—one that will take you six months

> *Make sure that you always follow your heart and your gut, and let yourself be who you want to be, and who you know you are. And don't let anyone steal your joy."*
>
> — Jonathan Groff

> *I think it's imperative to follow your heart and choose a profession you're passionate about, and if you haven't found that 'spark' yet, if you're not sure what you want to do with your lives - be persistent until you do."*
>
> — Steve Kerr

or one that will take you 10 years—it may be a good idea to consider pursuing the more easily accomplished of the two first. This will allow you to get a taste of success and from there you can continue on to the more difficult goal.

However, when you are faced with two alternatives and all other things are equal, I would suggest that you pursue the one that is most appealing to you. The reason for this is simple: you need passion to pursue your goals. Passion is what gives birth to grit and tenacity. If you are pursuing a goal because you truly want to accomplish it, then you will have a much higher level of determination and perseverance than you would if you were pursuing a goal that you were not as passionate about.

When I say to follow your heart, I do not mean it that you should necessarily discount every other consideration. Sometimes it is more prudent to pursue an option that is more achievable first before you pursue the one about which you are truly passionate. This is because success is cyclical: the more success that you enjoy, the more drive and perseverance you will have; the more drive and perseverance you have the more you'll be able to achieve your goals. For this reason, I do suggest choosing a more readily accomplished goal over something that will take you significantly longer (although you should note I am not saying that you should abandon the latter goal; simply that you may want to consider pursuing a shorter-term goal first).

Now, when I say to follow your heart, I mean that you should let your passion be the deciding factor in a situation where all other things are equal between two alternatives. This simply makes sense because without passion, you will either quit when you become discouraged or you'll become bored and simply give up.

On the other hand, if you're passionate about your chosen goal, you will not find yourself so easily drawn from its pursuit. As you'll find over the coming months and years, passion is something without which you will have a difficult time moving on. Passion will give rise to the grit which you need to pick yourself up when things get tough. Passion will help you to persevere in the face of adversity and to continue working—no matter how difficult things may seem—until you reach the goal to which you aspire.

I challenge you to take a look around you as you go about your daily life. Observe the people with whom you interact and consider their level of passion for what they are doing. You will notice that the ones who seem most excited about what they are doing are also the ones who tend to be the most successful. On the other hand, the ones who are simply there for a paycheck or because they are being otherwise forced to perform a certain task will be the ones who are wallowing in mediocrity and do not take very much pride in what they do. This attitude will of course be reflected in the quality of work that they perform.

You do not want to be like that when you are pursuing your goals. Your goals should excite and challenge you so that you are excited each day when it is time for you to spend some time pursuing them. This is not to say that there will not be days that you want to quit. It is simply human nature to sometimes grow tired and discouraged when things are not going the way that we think they should. However, if you are passionate about your end goal, this passion will carry you through those times of temporary discouragement.

So, when choosing between two alternatives, consider how quickly you may achieve each one and—if there is a tremendous amount of difference between the two—you may want to consider pursuing the goal which would be more easily accomplished simply because this accomplishment will give you more confidence on which to build. (Of course, if you are extremely, extremely passionate about one goal and not that excited about the other one, then you may want to consider pursuing the goal about which you are passionate, even if that goal is the one which will take longer to accomplish.)

If the two alternatives will take a similar amount of time to accomplish then I would definitely suggest that you choose the one that pulls at your heartstrings more. Following your heart can definitely help you to reach your goals.

> *One may walk over the highest mountain one step at a time.*
> — John Wanamaker

Regarding the matter of facing a large task, I have found that the easiest way is to approach it one step at a time. It is easy to become overwhelmed when you are faced with the prospect of climbing a mountain; on the other hand, if you are only considering taking five or six steps forward suddenly the task seems much more possible. And yet, as John Wanamaker so aptly pointed out, the way to climb a mountain is simply one step at a time.

When you divide a large task up into smaller tasks it seems much more manageable. In addition to that, it gives you something to celebrate along the way. When you take each small portion of the goal and treat each one as if it—in and of itself—is a goal, you will find that your spirits are lifted as you accomplish each one of your goals along the way towards your main goal. This is a psychological benefit, but it will really make a difference in your experience.

I actually knew one person who climbed mountains as a hobby and one cardinal rule he had was this: once the climb has started, you only look so far

> *To get through the hardest journey we need take only one step at a time, but we must keep on stepping.*
> — Chinese Proverb

ahead as is necessary for your safety. He implemented this rule because when he was a novice climber, he made the mistake of looking all the way up to where he was trying to go. He told me that when he did that he could feel the resolution and determination melting away from within him.

> *"Very often, what is meant to be a stepping stone turns out to be a slab of wet cement that will harden around your foot if you do not take the next step soon enough."*
>
> Richelle E. Goodrich, *Making Wishes: Quotes, Thoughts, & a Little Poetry for Every Day of the Year*

From then on, he would only look as far ahead as was necessary for his own safety so that he would not repeat that tragic mistake. After that, it was relatively easy for him to complete his climbs because—as he himself told me—a huge part of conquering something as overwhelming as a mountain is simply keeping yourself motivated to keep taking one step at a time.

I knew a college student who was working full time and pursuing two different graduate degrees at the same time. He told me that each semester, he would sit down with his calendar and divide up the semester into chunks. Then, he would further divide each chunk into one-week periods.

He would celebrate the completion of each week. After four weeks had passed than he would celebrate the completion of a chunk of the semester. This was how he got through the semester: one day at a time. He told me that if he had sat down and considered how far away the end of each semester was he very likely would have dropped out of school all together.

One step at a time is the best way to approach the seemingly overwhelming tasks. Each step is necessary to get there: you cannot take the journey of 1000 miles, if you do not take step number one, step number two, step number three, and so on. Each step—while by itself seemingly an insignificant action—is a required part of completing the journey.

So you need to focus just on the next step. Further, when you do accomplish the next step, you need to celebrate that. Celebrating it will help you to realize the significance of each stage of your journey and, in addition, will help you keep your spirits lifted by reminding you that you are one stage closer to your ultimate goal.

At the same time, while you are celebrating, don't become content and sit back on your laurels. If you do that, you may find that it is difficult to get up again. This is the reason I included the last quote above: to remind you to keep moving forward no matter what. You should celebrate your accomplishments, but you should not become complacent. Rather, you need to set your mind on your ultimate goal and keep pushing forward.

Conclusion

It can be difficult when deciding between multiple goals to pursue. In such a situation where you are overwhelmingly pulled towards one goal instead of the other, then of course you should follow your desire. On the other hand, if there is not a huge disparity in your passion between the two alternatives, you may want to consider tackling the easier of the two first. This will give you an added boost in morale when you turn towards the more difficult goal.

On the other hand, if the two goals seem to be about the same as far as the amount of time and difficulty it will be to accomplish each one, you should definitely follow your heart. Following your heart will keep you passionate about your goal; passion will keep you moving forward when you might otherwise be tempted to quit.

Finally, when it comes to a large task, the best way to handle it is one step at a time. Don't let yourself become overwhelmed by the size of the mountain in front of you; rather, simply determine to take one step. And then take another. And then take another. Each step is important, and each step will get you closer to the ultimate goal. Don't forget to celebrate each accomplishment along the way, and do not underestimate the importance of taking each step.

CHAPTER 8

AUGUST: CHANGE REQUIRES CHANGE

Question: All my life I have been something of a pessimist. For a long time, I disputed this notion, instead claiming that I was simply a realist, but I am finally starting to accept the fact that I tend to have a negative outlook on life. I would like to change this—I really would—and I have tried to push the negative thoughts out of my mind, but the moment I forget to do this they start to creep back in. Most of my negativity seems to be centered on my belief that I'm simply not good enough to be much of a success in life. I feel like I'm not as intelligent or talented as I need to be in order to be a success. Further, I find that because I hold these beliefs, I tend to not even try to succeed because I feel like it's pointless to even attempt it when I know what the ultimate outcome will be.

I am not at all happy with being this way, but I just don't know what I can do about it. As I said I have tried to push my negative thoughts away, but they always seem to creep back in when I'm not looking. Can you help me?

Absolutely, I can help you and I'm glad that you brought this concern to me. It is one thing to try to think "positive thoughts" in order to counter too many negative thoughts; it is something else entirely to actually reprogram the way that you think about things and approach life. I am going to help you reprogram the way that you think.

In my book *Essential Assertions,* I spend a couple of chapters discussing the matter of believing in yourself because what you believe about yourself will eventually become your experience. Your thoughts about what you are will drive what you become. The following excerpt from my book tells a story that illustrates this point. I have shortened it a little bit from the way it appears in that book, but I think you will still get the point.

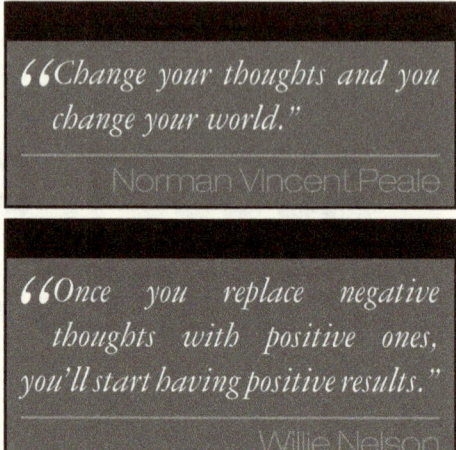

> Once upon a time there was a small worm. He lived much as worms do: crawling around, eating leaves, and trying to avoid being eaten by spiders.
>
> As time went by, he would occasionally look and dream about flying. Oh, to be able to fly! To be able to just fly away when a spider approached!
>
> He shared this hope with a few ants he knew. Their response was to laugh and say, "You are a worm. You'd better quit wasting time dreaming of impossibilities and find a good hiding place because that spider is heading over here!"
>
> So the worm went and hid. As he was hiding, he contemplated the conversation. *I suppose it's true, I'm just a worm. I really can't do anything else besides crawl around and hide from spiders. I better forget about flying and just concentrate on surviving.*

As time passed and the worm grew fatter he would occasionally see a butterfly in the sky. He would think *That must be nice, but that's just how life goes: some are born with all the luck and get to fly, and some are born without luck and must crawl. I'm just a worm and I can't fly so I'm going to forget about it.*

Eventually, as worms are known to do, the worm made a nice bed for himself by means of spinning a cocoon. He snuggled down and as he was drifting off to sleep he thought *I'm just a worm. I'll just be content to crawl around on the ground.*

As the worm slept, he sprouted wings. When he awoke and clambered out of his cocoon, he saw a nice juicy leaf off in the distance. Hungry, he began to walk toward it. As he walked, he thought *I'm just a worm. I am happy with my lot in life.*

As he neared the leaf, a shadow fell over him. A large spider had entered the area and was devouring everything in its path. A few ants ran past, yelling at him, "You better fly away!" The butterfly sighed and said, "I wish I could, but I'm just a worm. I better go find a hiding place!" And then he ran away to hide under a rock.

This story—admittedly somewhat silly—illustrates a very crucial point: *what you believe about yourself will drive your experience.* I am belaboring this point because I want to underscore the importance of reprogramming your thinking. If you think that you are only a worm then you will have the experience of a worm regardless of the wings sprouting out of your back; on the other hand, if you believe that you can fly, then you will find a way to make it happen regardless of what other people may say about you.

The point, then, is this: you must change the way that you think about yourself in order for you to change the types of experiences you are having in your life. Again, I repeat: *what you believe about yourself will drive your experience.*

Because it is so important to alter what you think about yourself I am going to spend the second half of this chapter discussing a method for changing the way that you think. Although you might think that it is silly, I simply ask you to bear with me and give it a try. Try the exercise I will share with you for 30 days and you will see that it really does make a difference in your attitude and your experience.

> *"Great thoughts come from the heart."*
> Luc de Clapiers

In my book *Essential Assertions,* I devote an entire chapter (chapter 4, if you are interested in reading it) to discussing the matter of engaging in positive visualization exercises; I do this because these exercises are crucial in shaping your experience. I call it visionerring . . .

Basically, a visualization exercise is an exercise in which you take some time, clear your thoughts, and begin to envision yourself succeeding. This visualization exercise should be as detailed as you can make it. For example, if your goal is to earn enough money to build your dream home, then in your visualization exercises you should take yourself on a mental tour of your new home.

You should go from room to room, examining all the fixtures; the carpeting; the furnishings; and so on. You should spend time in each room taking in all of the details and considering how wonderful it is going to be when this visualization actually becomes your experience.

You should spend time in each room and envision exactly the way it is going to be. Pay attention to even the finest details such as the type of faucet in the kitchen or the pattern of the title that you will lay down or even the type of drapery that you will have.

Be sure to take time to admire the beautiful hardwood floors and the granite countertops. You should even pay attention to the brass electrical outlet covers. Take a walk out onto your back deck and spend some time admiring the landscaping you have in your backyard. Perhaps you will have a fish pond with some colorful Koi fish; perhaps you will have a stone patio underneath a pergola with beautiful magnolia vines growing up and flowering in the canopy above the patio.

The point here is to be as detailed in your visualization as you possibly can be. The more time you spend doing this, the more you will begin to truly believe that you are going to make that home your own. Eventually, your experience will match your vision.

The concept of engaging in a visualization exercise is not limited to material things such as a new home. Whatever your goal is, you can spend time engaging in visualization exercises regarding it. Perhaps your goal is to become a more outgoing conversationalist. So, you can visualize it: close your eyes and imagine going to a social gathering. Instead of cowering in the corner waiting for your first chance to escape, visualize yourself going from person to person engaging in light hearted banter. Visualize the response that people will have when they see you approaching and the way that they will laugh when you tell a funny story. By visualizing yourself being a successful conversationalist you will eventually find that you are a successful conversationalist!

> *A positive attitude causes a chain reaction of positive thoughts, events and outcomes. It is a catalyst and it sparks extraordinary results."*
> — Wade Boggs

Whatever you want to be, simply spend time visualizing this, and eventually you will become the thing you are envisioning. This exercise is used by people in all walks of life. Professional athletes use it to help them perform at the next level. For example, many golfers visualize the perfect swing and the perfect drive from the tee. Doing this helps them to achieve and maintain perfect form. By visualizing the perfect swing, they find that they are training muscle memory so that when they actually step out on the course the swing comes naturally.

Again I say: this technique is not limited to physical things such as a house or even the best form when swinging a golf club. You can use this technique to visualize yourself being successful at whatever it is you currently consider yourself to be unsuccessful.

I would encourage you to engage in visualization exercises several times a day. Instead of waiting to catch yourself thinking negative thoughts and then trying to counteract those thoughts, you should instead, develop the habit of engaging in positive visualization exercises. Over time you will find yourself believing that you can do it without even thinking about trying to "think positive thoughts." At that point you will know that the visualization exercises are working and are assisting you in counteracting the negative thoughts that you have learned to entertain.

Conclusion

What you think about yourself is very important because your view of yourself will actually drive your experience in life. Because of this it is extremely important that you learn how to overcome your habit of entertaining negative thoughts. However, it is not sufficient simply to resolve that you will no longer think negative thoughts, or to decide that you are only going to think positive thoughts. Such an endeavor will only last for as long as you remember to do it.

Instead of trying to fight your negative thoughts you need to develop the habit of engaging in positive visualization exercises on a regular basis. Spend time imagining yourself succeeding at whatever task it is you currently struggle with. Your visualizations should be as detailed as you can make them; in your mind it should actually feel like you are doing whatever it is that you are visualizing.

By engaging in regular positive visualization exercises you will be re-training your brain to think only positive thoughts. This is important because—as your question reveals—currently your brain is trained to think many negative things about yourself. So, just as with any other habit, you need to implement a habit to counteract the "negative thinking" habit you have developed. Positive visualization exercises done on a regular basis—at least three or four times a day—will eventually become a habit and out of this habit will flow positive thinking.

Once you have the habit of engaging in positive thinking you will find that—more and more frequently—your experience matches with your vision. It really does matter what you believe about yourself and what you believe about your capabilities. So you need to train your brain to think positive thoughts and believe only good things about yourself. Once you do this you are well on the way to enjoying the successful life you have always desired.

CHAPTER 9

SEPTEMBER: FAITH MATTERS

Question: I grew up in a house where faith was emphasized. However, as I've grown older, I have kind of lost my faith. Don't get me wrong: I still believe in a Creator. However, I'm no longer sure that it even really matters whether I believe or not. I mean, it seems like regardless of whether I believe or not my life is pretty much the same. Do you have any advice for me?

I am glad to hear that you have not completely lost your faith. Further, I would say that it does in fact matter whether you have faith or not because—as we have discussed before—when it comes to the matter of your success in achieving your goals, your mindset is one of the most important factors in the equation. A strong sense of faith will help you approach your obstacles with a positive mindset; as such, I would say that faith is actually quite important in the overall scheme of things.

Because faith is instrumental in helping you to achieve and maintain a positive mindset, and because a positive mindset is crucial in assisting you to reach your goals, it naturally follows that faith is an important part of reaching your goals. While I suppose you could make the argument that there are some people out there who reject the notion of a Creator, and yet *they* are still successful in reaching their goals, I would counter that by pointing out that even those people have faith in *something:* their own abilities and talents.

I want to begin by discussing what faith is, exactly, and what it does for you in your everyday experience. Faith is that ability to believe—whether you believe in the existence of the Creator, your own abilities, or something else. If you believe in something, then you are demonstrating faith. This is why there are many people who do not believe in the Creator, and yet they still are able to be successful in their endeavors: they still have faith in something (themselves and their abilities).

> "Faith is the substance of hope—of things hoped for and the evidence of things not seen. So if you can hope for it and imagine it, and keep imagining and hoping and seeing yourself driving a new car, or seeing yourself getting that job, or seeing yourself excel, seeing yourself help that person—that is faith."
>
> Duane Chapman

Think about this for a moment. If you do not believe that something is possible, then you will most likely not even bother trying to get there. After all, if the outcome will be the same regardless of whether you try or not, why would you bother putting in the time and effort to even try reaching your goals?

Because you will never reach your goals if you do not try to get there, and because you will not try to get there unless you believe that you can get there, it is important that you believe in something. This is faith. Without faith, you will never reach your goals because you will never even start down the path towards them.

Further, regarding the matter of those who do not believe in the Creator and yet believe in themselves, I would posit that in a sense they actually *are* exercising faith in the Creator. Here's why: when the Creator created you, he put his life in you. You are his creation;

his creature. Because the life that is in you has its source in the Creator, then when you believe in his life you are believing in him.

Worded differently, believing in the Creator and believing in yourself are actually two sides of the same coin because as the Creator's creation you possess his life within you. Thus, when you believe in yourself, you are believing in the life that pulses within your being—the same life that the Creator gave you—and whether you realize it or not you are indirectly believing in the Creator. In short, you are exercising faith.

> *"Pray as though everything depended on God. Work as though everything depended on you."*
> — Saint Augustine

Now I would like to spend some time discussing why it is so important that you have faith. I briefly touched upon one reason in the above section (namely, the idea that if you do not have faith you will not believe you can accomplish your goals, and if you do not believe that you can accomplish your goals, you will never bother beginning, and if you never bother to begin then you will of course never finish).

However, there is an additional reason why it is important for you to have faith: your faith will not only enable you to begin the arduous journey towards accomplishing your goal, but it will also make that journey bearable and even enjoyable, and it will allow you to continue moving towards your goals once obstacles begin to arise.

To put this differently, the reason for having faith that I mentioned in the above section deals with *beginning* your journey towards your goals; the reason that I will now discuss deals with *continuing*

> *"God, our Creator, has stored within our minds and personalities, great potential strength and ability. Prayer helps us tap and develop these powers."*
> — A. P. J. Abdul Kalam

that journey in the face of difficult developments. And, as I have mentioned before, any goal that is worth accomplishing will inevitably involve overcoming some difficulties.

So, regarding your exercise of faith and how it affects your ongoing journey towards your goals, consider the story of the little engine that could. First published in 1930, this story is a classic illustration of the power of believing in yourself and putting your head down, gritting up, and deciding to keep moving forward no matter what.

In the unlikely event that you are unfamiliar with the story here is an abbreviated version:

> A little railroad engine was employed about a station yard for such work as it was built for, pulling a few cars on and off the switches. One morning it was waiting for the next call when a long train of freight-cars asked a large engine in the roundhouse to take it over the hill. "I can't; that is too much a pull for me," said the great engine built for hard work. Then the train asked another engine, and another, only to hear excuses and be refused. In desperation, the train asked the little switch engine to draw it up the grade and down on the other side. "I think I can," puffed the little locomotive, and put itself in front of the great heavy train. As it went on the little engine kept bravely puffing faster and faster, "I think I can, I think I can, I think I can."
>
> As it neared the top of the grade, which had so discouraged the larger engines, it went more slowly. However, it still kept saying, "I—think—I—can, I—think—I—can." It reached the top by drawing on bravery and then went on down the grade, congratulating itself by saying, "I thought I could, I thought I could."[2]

Longer versions of the story emphasize the little engine's grit and determination. As the little engine climbed the hill, its progress slowed down until it barely inched along. Yet, in spite of the difficult

---

[2] Wikipedia.org (website). The Little Engine that Could. Available at https://en.wikipedia.org/wiki/The_Little_Engine_That_Could. Last visited November 30, 2015.

climb in front of it, and in spite of the fact that it was barely making any progress, the little engine kept repeating to itself "I think I can." Each time it repeated this phrase of self-affirmation it progressed a tiny bit further up the hill.

The little engine had faith in itself; likewise, you should have faith in yourself. You may wonder what this has to do with having faith in the Creator. Well, consider Psalm 139:14, which says, ". . . I am fearfully and wonderfully made." When you believe in the Creator you will also believe his words as written in the Bible. These words can become a great source of encouragement and inspiration because they reveal what the Creator himself thinks about you: and he thinks very highly indeed of you!

So you see, having faith in the Creator will in turn lead to more faith in yourself. As you begin to consider the Creator and all of his marvelous work in creation, then you begin to see just what an amazing creation you yourself are. As you begin to realize what a marvelous work of art you are, you will likewise begin to appreciate yourself more, and you will begin to believe in your own abilities and talents more.

Having faith in the Creator leads to having faith in his creation (that's you!). Increased faith in yourself will, in turn, lead to a heightened determination to continue towards your goal, even if it means fighting for one step at a time. Just like the little engine that could, you will be ready to repeat words of self-affirmation and fight with all of your might to take just one more little step. And then one more little step after that. And then one more little step after that. And so on. Of course, as you know from the story, the culmination of all these little steps toward your goal eventually will be reaching the top of the "hill" you are climbing.

Conclusion

Having faith is an important part of your journey towards your goal. If you do not have faith, then you will not believe in anything that you do not see with your own two eyes. This means you will have a more difficult time believing that you can ever reach your goals. Because you'll be less likely to believe in your ability to reach your goals, you will also be less likely to even start on your journey towards them. And—because you can never finish a journey that you do not first start—you will be much less likely to ever reach your goals.

Remember that the life which is in you is the life which has its source in the Creator. Thus, in a sense, having faith in the Creator is having faith in his life; having faith in his life is having faith in the very life which resides within your being. Having faith in the Creator and having faith in yourself are two sides to the same coin.

Likewise, it is important to exercise your faith in the Creator because you are his creation! When you begin to have faith in the Creator, then you begin to see what he thinks about you as is written in the Bible. The Bible shows that the Creator thinks very highly of his creation (you!). Knowing this is an incredible boost to your morale and will encourage you to pick yourself up off the ground and keep on trying when you encounter difficulties. Much like the little engine that could, you will keep pushing forward one step at a time as you grow ever closer towards the realization of your dreams and goals. This will make your daily experiences bearable and enjoyable as you inch closer to your destination.

CHAPTER 10

OCTOBER: MINDSET

Question: When I was younger, I had a dream. I tried to reach my dream and failed; the cost of my failure was quite high. Now, a few decades later, I still have that dream, and I would like to reach for it again, but I'm afraid of what may happen if I fail. Is there anything you can tell me that would help with my fear?

First, I want to help you become clear on what it is that fear does to you. In your case, it prevents you from reaching for your goal. Second, I want to discuss the issue of why you are afraid (you're afraid of failure) and why this is unnecessary (because you cannot truly fail). Third, I want to give you some practical advice on ways to handle your fear.

> *"Fear keeps us focused on the past or worried about the future. If we can acknowledge our fear, we can realize that right now we are okay. Right now, today, we are still alive, and our bodies are working marvelously. Our eyes can still see the beautiful sky. Our ears can still hear the voices of our loved ones."*
>
> Thich Nhat Hanh

I would like to start out by discussing what fear does to you; or, more accurately, what it does to your potential for greatness. When you are afraid you tend to withdraw and take fewer risks. On the one hand, this is a nifty survival mechanism; on the other, this prevents you from setting out on your journey towards greatness.

> "We consume our tomorrows fretting about our yesterdays."
> —Persius

When you are so consumed with what happened yesterday that it keeps you from acting today to change tomorrow, that fear has become a problem. It has become more than a mere act of self-preservation. Instead, it has become an obstacle that hamstrings you on your journey to success.

Fear prevents you from being great for the simple fact that in order to be great you have to journey towards that greatness, and fear keeps you from setting foot outside of your safe zone. Do you want to live a life that is unremarkable in every way? Do you want to come to the end of your days with all your dreams unrealized and filled with thoughts of *What would have happened if I had. . . ?* Do you want to leave nothing worthwhile behind you? Then be safe. Focusing on being safe and avoiding all risk is the best way I know of to ensure that you will never reach greatness.

I'm not saying that prudence is a liability; on the contrary, if we never took time to calculate the least risky course of action to reach a given result our days would be filled with havoc and chaos. Quite likely the human race would have fallen prey to some catastrophe by this point if we had never learned to act with prudence.

But there is a key difference between being prudent and being controlled by your fear. When you are prudent, you determine to reach a certain result with the least amount of risk that is possible; when you are controlled by your fear, you determine to avoid risk at all costs—even at the cost of giving up your goals. Do you see the distinction?

Put differently, prudence is moving ahead towards your goal while doing what is reasonably possible to minimize the risk to yourself; being fearful is refusing to move towards your goal unless all risk is eliminated (which will never happen, by the way).

> *"What is needed, rather than running away or controlling or suppressing or any other resistance, is understanding fear; that means, watch it, learn about it, come directly into contact with it. We are to learn about fear, not how to escape from it."*
> — Jiddu Krishnamurti

I'm not telling you that you should not be prudent; rather, I'm telling you that you should not be fearful. Every worthwhile accomplishment known to man has involved some level of risk. If you are so afraid to fail that it paralyzes you from even *trying* to succeed, then that is a problem.

Now, I want to briefly touch upon why you are afraid. You are afraid because you have some unpleasant memories associated with trying to reach your goals, and you would like to avoid a repeat of those experiences. While this is understandable, it also reflects a lack of understanding on your part.

First, this state of mind suggests a belief that you can reach your goals without paying a price. This is simply wrong. Every goal that is worth your effort is going to require the paying of a price to reach. Whether that price is in your sweat, your tears, or even your blood, there will be a price to pay.

You need to accept this fact so that you can then resolve within yourself to simply pay the price for success. Do not be lulled into thinking that you can have success without paying for it; success is a precious thing, and the price for it is quite high. This is not to say it's not worth it—on the contrary, few things in life are as worthwhile as chasing your dreams—but it is to say that

> *"True success is overcoming the fear of being unsuccessful."*
> — Paul Sweeney

you need to have your eyes opened as to the nature of success and realize that reaching it does entail the paying of a price.

The mindset that you would like to avoid repeating your earlier experiences also shows a lack of understanding of what it truly means to fail. As I have discussed earlier in this book, failure is not defined as obtaining an outcome besides the one you were hoping for. Rather, failure is when you don't give your best effort at reaching your goal and you learn nothing from the experience.

If you try to reach your goal and you fall short but—in the process—you learn a valuable lesson that can then be applied to your next endeavor, then that's *not a failure!* Rather, it is simply a part of the learning process. You have learned a lesson that will take you one step closer to ultimately achieving your goal. Thus, the experience—unpleasant as it may be—is simply the price you pay for moving closer to your goals and dreams.

You need to view your past experience in light of what we have discussed here, namely that (1) every goal which is worthwhile will have a price that must be paid; and (2) an outcome other than the one you were expecting and/or hoping for is *never a failure if you learned something.* Using this measure, take a new look at your past experience. Do you still consider it to be a failure? Most likely not, assuming that you learned something from the whole experience which you can now apply in your future attempts. Further, given that you must pay a price to succeed, do you still wish to avoid similar experiences in the future? Hopefully not; not if you have seen the true value of success and realize that something so precious will always carry with it a price that must be paid.

> *"Fear can be good when you're walking past an alley at night or when you need to check the locks on your doors before you go to bed, but it's not good when you have a goal and you're fearful of obstacles. We often get trapped by our fears, but anyone who has had success has failed before."*
>
> Queen Latifah

Finally, I want to spend a few moments giving you some practical advice regarding your fear and what you can do in order to be freed from it. Hopefully, you understand from the first part of our discussion that fear is something more than merely being prudent. I would never encourage you to not act prudently; however, I will always encourage you to not be bound by fear.

Fear prevents you from being great, because fear prevents you from trying to reach your goals. You will never go anywhere if you don't at least try. And so you see that fear is actually far more damaging than a situation where you do not realize the outcome for which you had hoped.

If you at least try to reach your goals, then you'll come one step closer to doing so even if the outcome of that particular attempt isn't quite what you had hoped for. On the other hand, if you don't even try then you'll never come any closer to greatness.

So, what can you do in order to deal with fear and prevent it from causing you to freeze up instead of act when the time comes? Well, for one thing, remember what I said about success having a price. If you understand this, and if you make peace with paying that price, then you won't ever fear a situation where you don't achieve your goal because you will understand and accept that these situations are (1) merely part of the price you pay to ultimately reach your goals; and (2) a necessary step in the process towards your ultimate success.

In fact, if you can begin to see these scenarios (scenarios in which you don't "fail" but you do end up with an outcome other than the one for which you were hoping) as steps in the process, you will actually end up treasuring them because each one brings you one footstep closer to your goal.

So the first thing to do in order to overcome your fear is to understand the true nature of these experiences in which your outcome is not the one you had desired. These experiences are both a part of the price you pay and a step in the process that will eventually lead to your success. When viewed in this light, these experiences no longer feel like a failure and they do not seem as troublesome because we understand both their necessity and even their value in the overall process of success.

The next thing you can do in order to deal with fear is simply make the resolution within yourself that you are going to grit up and keep trying time after time after time. Once you have made this determination, then you won't be bothered by an outcome other than the one you were hoping for because you'll know that it's "just another day at the office." You won't even be bothered by it because you will have already made the determination—deep within your being—that you're going to come back the next day, buckle down, and keep working.

If you do this—and you do this faithfully over the course of your lifetime—you will find yourself accomplishing goal after goal. It will truly become your experience that nothing is too large for you; no task is impossible when you truly set your will to it.

By taking these steps you can reduce the impact fear has on you. This, in turn, will free you from the paralysis that all too frequently accompanies fear. Remember, the biggest thing that fear does is prevent us from ever becoming better because we are too afraid of failing to even bother trying.

Conclusion

Fear prevents you from ever trying to reach your goal; thus fear ensures failure because you—by definition—can never reach a goal to which you did not aspire. Thus, you must find a way to be freed from your fear if you are ever to have any hope of reaching your goals.

You are afraid of repeating your earlier experiences because you do not truly understand the process of becoming a success. Remember two things: (1) success comes only with a price; and (2) outcomes other than the ones you planned for are not failures so long as you gave it everything you had and learned something that you can apply to your future endeavors. If you remember these things, then the experience of obtaining an outcome besides that for which you were hoping will not be so bothersome because you will realize that (1) the situation is simply part of the price you pay; and (2) the situation itself is precious because it brings you one step closer to your ultimate success.

Finally, to be freed from your fear you need to not only understand the process of becoming a success; you also need to make the determination that you are going to buckle down and keep working no matter what happens. You must decide that you will grit up and persevere even in the face of adversity. If you make this determination, then an unexpected outcome from your efforts will not deter you; you'll view it as simply another step in the process and you'll return the next day, primed and ready to keep working towards your goals.

CHAPTER 11

NOVEMBER: PERSPECTIVE IS EVERYTHING

Question: I have a moderately successful career, fairly good health, and a good family. I should be thankful, but I keep looking at the lives of my peers from college and wondering why my life could not have turned out like theirs. They have it all: great jobs, health, and families that are perfect. How can I stop looking at those who have it better than I do and instead simply be grateful for what I have?

First, I would like to suggest to you that it's quite likely your peers do not have the perfect life you may think they do. Regarding their *perfect* families, you don't see what goes on behind closed doors. Further, regarding their apparent material success, many people are not nearly as successful as they let on. They may drive new, expensive cars and live in large, opulent houses, but it is very likely that they are up to their eyeballs in debt trying to keep up the façade. I would be very reluctant to classify anyone as a success simply because you see them putting up pictures of their new car on their social media account or whatever.

Having said that, even if they *are* as successful as you think they are, you still should be happy for the blessings that you have been given. It is an unfortunate part of human nature to look longingly at those things which we do not have while ignoring those things we already do have. Consider this: if an unemployed homeless person living in a shelter somewhere were able to take a look at your current position, do you think that he or she would trade places with you if the opportunity were offered to them? I think, in a heartbeat, their answer would be "yes!" Yet, even they themselves likely do not realize how good they have it compared to, for example, a homeless orphan in a 3rd world country who sleeps on the streets and digs through garbage cans for sustenance.

Being content with your position is a matter of perspective. If you only see the things that you do not have, you will never be happy. On the other hand, if you gratefully consider all the blessings that you have been given, you will find that happiness is yours even if you don't drive the most expensive car or live in the largest house. It's all in how you look at your position in life.

> *"A grateful heart is a beginning of greatness. It is an expression of humility. It is a foundation for the development of such virtues as prayer, faith, courage, contentment, happiness, love, and well-being."*
>
> — James E. Faust

I'd like to spend a few minutes talking about what it is that being grateful does for you. Being grateful for what you have and the blessings that you have been given is one thing that will save you from becoming entitled and arrogant. We have all seen small children throw a temper tantrum when they aren't given what they want; then, after they are given whatever it is they want, they act as if it was something that they had a *right* to have rather than being something for which they should be grateful.

Sad to say, many adults are the same way, even today. They expect that certain things in life are a right and something to which they are entitled. If they don't have an expensive car, a nice house, or great health, they sit around complaining. As if the world owes them these things and they are being affronted by not receiving them.

We've all known people who were blessed with a nice car (or whatever) and because they weren't grateful they seemed to think that such a car was their birthright. These types of people tend to be arrogant and look down on other people who are not as fortunate. At the other end of the spectrum, we've all known people who didn't have a nice car and instead of being happy that at least they had *some* form of transportation they spent their time complaining and whining about how unfair life is. Neither type of person is someone that you want to be around.

> *"I believe that if you don't derive a deep sense of purpose from what you do, if you don't come radiantly alive several times a day, if you don't feel deeply grateful at the tremendous good fortune that has been bestowed on you, then you are wasting your life. And life is too short to waste."*
>
> Srikumar Rao

Being grateful will save you from acting this way. When you get that expensive car, you will be happy that you got it and not look down on others who don't have it; on the other hand, if you for some reason never do get that expensive car, you will still be happy that at least you have a car and you don't have to take the bus or walk everywhere. In either event—whether you get the car or not—maintaining an air of gratefulness will help you to remain humble, happy, and loving towards others. It will make you a more pleasant person to be around, and it will actually make you *happier* with your lot in life.

> ❝Be *thankful for what you have; you'll end up having more. If you concentrate on what you don't have, you will never, ever have enough.*"
>
> — Oprah Winfrey

Being grateful not only makes you happier and a more pleasant person to be around, it is also a self-reinforcing cycle. Consider the way our mind works: if you are happy with where you are in life you are more likely to see things that happen to you as a positive. Inversely, if you are unhappy with your position and ungrateful for your blessings, you will see things that happen as a negative, even when they are in fact a positive.

Let's use an illustration. Let's say that someone gives you a used car. This car is in reasonably good shape and should serve to transport you from place to place without any problems. This car does have a scratch in the paint where someone accidentally dropped something on the hood.

> ❝*Do not indulge in dreams of having what you have not, but reckon up the chief of the blessings you do possess, and then thankfully remember how you would crave for them if they were not yours.*"
>
> — Marcus Aurelius, *Meditations*

Now, if you are a grateful person you will react with happiness, glad that you got a new car! On the other hand, if the only thing you can see is how bad you have it in life, then if you are given that same car your response is more likely to be along the lines of, "Great, now I've got to spend money to fix this scratch. Why couldn't I have gotten a brand-new car like my neighbor? *He always* gets *everything.*"

Do you see the distinction here? In both cases you got a new car, and you got it for free! If you are grateful for your position in life you will automatically register this as a positive and you will be happy. If you are ungrateful, you will focus on the negative and actually find yourself complaining about getting a free car. This is just how our mind works. If you're grateful and happy, you will put a positive spin on things. If you're ungrateful, you won't.

You've heard the expression "Looking through rose-colored glasses." This describes someone who is naturally happy and so everything they view has a rosy tint to it. Did you know that you can also put on a pair of *dark* colored glasses, so everything you see looks gloomy and sad? Life is a matter of perspective: if you are grateful, your perspective will tend towards rosy; if you are ungrateful, it will tend to be gloomy and dissatisfied.

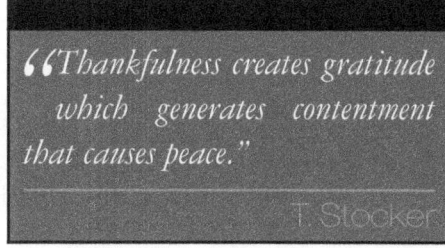

"Thankfulness creates gratitude which generates contentment that causes peace."

T. Stocker

Do you want to be happy in life? Of course you do! So, what is a practical step you can take towards happiness? Do you think that demanding more, more, more, and never being happy with the things you have been given will make you happy? Of course not! Yet, even though this seems so obvious as to be unworthy of mentioning it, by our attitudes and our actions we frequently seem to believe that we will reach happiness by being demanding.

How many times have you decided you wanted to get something—be it a new car, a nicer house, or whatever—and thought, "It will be so nice when I get that. *Then* I'll be happy."? And yet you find that, once you get that item, you're really not any happier than you were at the beginning?

"Gratitude paints little smiley faces on everything it touches."

Richelle E. Goodrich, *Smile Anyway: Quotes, Verse, & Grumblings for Every Day of the Year*

This is because happiness comes from your mindset, not from the possessions you have. If you are truly happy then you will be happy whether you're driving a brand-new Porsche or a used (but still serviceable) Ford. Happiness—true happiness—comes from realizing how many things you have to be thankful for and accepting each of your blessings with thanksgiving.

Rather than acting like a petulant child and receiving our blessings with a "But what about my neighbor? How come he gets a *better* car?!?" we should instead strive to be truly grateful for each and every blessing that comes to us. This will bring happiness, peace, and contentment.

Conclusion

It is easy to get into the mindset that you are owed a certain amount of blessings from life and that these blessings—when they come—had better be to a certain standard, or else. Unfortunately, this type of approach leads to more and more dissatisfaction. Instead of being happy with what you have, you instead compare yourself to someone else (who will inevitably have more than you) and complain about not having as much as that person.

A better way to approach life is to be truly grateful for each and every blessing, knowing that no matter how bad it may seem that you have it, there is always someone who is in worse shape than you are. Instead of complaining about the new car's scratch on the hood, be happy that you have a new car and you can drive to the store instead of trudging through the freezing rain. And, if you are that person who has to walk to the store through the rain, be happy that you have two legs and you can walk instead of being a paraplegic.

No matter how good you have it, someone else always has it better. No matter how bad you have it, someone else always has it worse. By keeping in mind that you are truly blessed, and being thankful for those things which you have been given, you will change your entire outlook on life. Your disposition will change, you will be more pleasant to be around, and you will be a happier person.

CHAPTER 12

DECEMBER: IT'S NEVER TOO LATE TO DREAM

Question: I have longed dreamed of starting my own business. I'm nearly 55 now, and I did start a business when I was 22. I worked at it for about six months, and I was making some headway towards becoming a successful small business owner, but then my wife became pregnant and I left the business to take a job that would provide more stability (as well as health insurance). I always intended to come back to my business, but one thing led to another and life got in the way. Now, nearing the end of my career, I'm considering returning to the business I started so many years ago. On the other hand, I'm starting to feel like it may be too late; maybe I'm too old. Do you have any advice?

I do have some advice for you. I think that you need to keep in mind the average lifespan of an adult in the U.S. is now more than 70 years, and with continuing advances in technology there's a good chance you'll live considerably longer than that. To that end, I don't think that you should let your age keep you from embarking on this journey. Let's take a closer look at your situation, and some of the things that you should be considering at this stage of your life and career.

> ❝Hold fast to dreams, for if dreams die, life is a broken winged bird that cannot fly."
> — Langston Hughes

> ❝The future belongs to those who believe in the beauty of their dreams."
> — Eleanor Roosevelt

> ❝Go confidently in the direction of your dreams. Live the life you have imagined."
> — Henry David Thoreau

> ❝Every great dream begins with a dreamer. Always remember, you have within you the strength, the patience, and the passion to reach for the stars to change the world."
> — Harriet Tubman

The first thing I want to talk about is following your dreams. I place a very heavy emphasis on this, as you can see by the fact that I selected four quotes on the topic. If you don't have a dream, you are little more than a mindless automaton trudging through life. You will get up in the morning, go to work, come home, spend a few pointless hours in the evening tinkering around with this or that, and then go to bed in the evening, only to get up the next day and do it all again. Over and over and over.

If you have no dreams, then you really have no direction in your life. Yes, you may have short-term directions (such as knowing that you have to go to work to make money to pay your bills) but you won't have any long-term direction. You will be like a ship drifting in the ocean: mindlessly moving in whatever direction the circumstances take you.

On the other hand, having a dream will give you a purpose for existing. It will impact every part of your life. No longer will you go to work simply to make money to pay the bills simply for the sake of keeping the bills paid; instead, you'll go to work to make money to pay the bills because keeping the bills paid is a necessary step to achieving your long-term goals. You will finally have a sense of purpose in doing what you do—even when you're doing the small mundane tasks associated with everyday living.

To have a dream is to have a purpose in your life. It is to infuse your existence with a sense of relevance. It is to give yourself something to work for instead of mindlessly existing simply because "that's the way things go." It will lift your morale because you will finally have a purpose, and it will infuse even your daily activities (such as going to work) with a deeper sense of accomplishment and even enjoyment.

So, my point is this: it's good to have a dream. It's good to have something you're looking forwards to other than simply the end of another workweek. I want you to dream. But a dream is no good if you're afraid to pursue it. If you have a dream of owning your own business but you're afraid—for whatever reason—to step out and pursue it, then the practical effect is no different than having no dream at all.

So, if you have a dream (and you have already told me that you do) then the next requirement is a willingness to step out and pursue that dream. I would like to take this opportunity to encourage you to pursue your dream because without your active pursuit thereof you may as well not even have a dream!

Regarding your concerns over your age, I will share with you something somebody once told me. I was in a situation where I was bemoaning my position and wishing that I had taken a certain course of action a number of years before. My friend was encouraging me to make the choice to pursue that course of action in spite of my perception that it was "too late" for me to go down that road. He said to me, "Rodney, today you are wishing that you had started a number of years ago. But you know what? A number of years from now you will wish that you had started today."

And he was right! You cannot turn back the clock and get a do-over on life. However, what you can do is make today the choices that you want to make, so that tomorrow you will not regret your inaction today. You may wish you had started 20 years ago; however, I would say to you that 20 years from now you will wish you had started today.

Your age should not be a consideration, unless it involves some physical limitations that make it impossible for you to (physically) perform the tasks you need to perform for your business. You did not communicate to me that this was the case; instead, I get the impression that you feel like it's too late because you're already (nearly) 55 and you seem to think that you'll not have enough years left in your life to enjoy the business if you start it today.

This mindset is the wrong way to look at things. Remember, life is a journey and not merely a destination. Your business is something you will enjoy when it's up and running, yes, but you'll also enjoy it during the process. The whole procedure from start to finish is something that will bring you joy and contentment. For that reason, I say go for it! Don't let fear—the fear that you will grow old and unable to enjoy the fruits of your labor before the business is ever a success—keep you rooted in your spot. If you launch your business today, it's true that you *might* not see it come to its ultimate peak;

however, it's equally true that if you don't launch your business, you *certainly* will not see your dreams become a reality. That old basketball adage is true: You miss 100% of the shots you don't take.

Even if the business takes 20 years to truly reach its potential, that 20 years can be a time of learning and enjoyment for you. There's no reason why you should hold back; rather, start today, so that 20 years from now you're not looking back and saying, "I wish I had started when I was 55."

I include this quote because it's interesting to me that you've come full circle: at the beginning of your professional life you embarked upon a journey with this business. You began to work towards building this business before some practical considerations caused you to switch paths in life.

> *"Th' hast spoken right, 'tis true. The wheel is come full circle, I am here."*
>
> William Shakespeare, King Lear, Act 5, scene 3, 171-175

That was at the beginning of your career. Now, towards the twilight of your career, you find yourself back in the position in which you were at the beginning. You find yourself standing in front of a door marked "Starting My Own Business" trying to determine whether you should open it and step through.

You cannot be sure what is behind this door: you could end up spending a significant amount of money and not ever seeing a return (at least not a financial one) or you could end up wealthy beyond your wildest dreams. Or, perhaps more likely, you may end up somewhere in between the two extremes.

Although there is an element of uncertainty to going through that door, I can tell you that you'll never know what could have been unless you do it. You can take the safe route and remain in your current position, never running the risk of going through that door. Or, you can reach deep down within your being, seize all the grit and determination you can muster, take a deep breath, and walk through the door. If you do this, although I cannot say for certain what the financial outcome can be, I can tell you that you will spend the next period of your life working towards something that you enjoy and feeling like you are making a difference in life.

At the beginning of your career you made the choice to put down your dream and do other things. That's a legitimate choice, and I'm not criticizing you for it. You weighed the pros and cons of each option and determined that—for you and for your young family—taking traditional employment was the best arrangement. Now, at the end of your career, you've come full circle. You once again have the opportunity to pick up your dream and move on towards your goal. I would encourage you to steel yourself, open the door, and walk through. Twenty years from now you will wish you had started today.

Conclusion

You need to have a dream to give your life some purpose and a sense of meaning. If you don't have a dream, then you are essentially just marking time until you die. You get up on Monday morning, go to work, come home and go to bed, only to repeat until Friday. Then you have a few precious days to yourself before starting it all again on Monday. This will be the cycle of your life unless you have some dream—some goal—that you can work towards.

It's good to have a goal, but merely having a goal does you no good unless you're moving towards it. If you have a dream, but you just set in on the shelf and never do anything with it, there's little difference between that and not having a dream at all.

You should determine within yourself to pursue your dream. And you should not allow your age to slow you down: you cannot turn back time, but you can make a choice to act today, so that tomorrow you will not regret what you did not do today.

You have come full circle in your life: from the beginning of your career when you were deciding whether to pursue your dream to the end of it when you find yourself again with the opportunity to seize your dreams. I would encourage you to grit up, take a deep breath, and walk through the door to your destiny.

AFTERWORD

Thank you for coming on this journey with me. I hope that you have found at least a few things along the way that will help you to become the success that you want to be. While these questions were taken from emails (or other communications) to me, I can tell you that several of them represent situations that I faced in my life. By following the principles laid out in my responses I was able to move past each issue and continue on my way down the path to success.

I want to take a moment to remind you that you are an incredible and unique person. Consider this: out of all the people who have ever existed on this planet, there is nobody else who is (or was) exactly the same as you are, with your exact blend of strengths and abilities. You are unique, and you are special.

Why do I emphasize this? Because I want to impress you with the monumental significance of your very existence. You are not a common occurrence; rather, like an exceedingly rare gemstone, you are a once in a lifetime event. Technically, you're even rarer than once in a lifetime; you are a once *in the history of the universe* event. Knowing this, you begin to understand on some level just how special and wonderful you are.

I tell you all this because I want to remind you that you are the culmination of hundreds and thousands of years of humanity. Consider all those who went before you: your parents, grandparents, great-grandparents, and so on. Stretching all the way back to the beginning of humanity. All those people in your lineage fought and worked in order that you could exist today.

You are a marvelous and wonderful creation, and you have within you the tools that you need to accomplish anything you set your mind to. Sit for a moment and imagine what you would like to do with your life. Do you want a bigger house? A better job? Your own business? Or maybe you want to be financially secure, such that you need not work at all?

Perhaps your goals are more altruistic: do you envision yourself starting a foundation to help those who are economically and socially disadvantaged? Perhaps you would like to run a charitable organization that provides food and shelter to those in need?

Whatever your goals, I want to be very clear with you: you have within your power the ability to accomplish them. The most powerful tools known to mankind are in your possession. I am of course speaking about your mind and your will. Whatever your goals, whatever your dreams, you can accomplish them if you set your will and choose to get there. All it takes is grit, perseverance, and determination.

I hope that the things you have read in these chapters will help you take a few shortcuts to addressing the various issues that you may encounter on your journey. However, as I'm sure you know, it would be impossible to write a single book that would address every single issue that every single reader will ever encounter.

At the end of the day, remember this one thing: You can do whatever you choose to do if you determine that you will not quit *no matter what happens*. If you make this determination, the rest is all just details.

Here's to your continued success. Now go out there and seize your dreams!

Rodney

ABOUT THE AUTHOR

Rodney Flowers is the Founder and President of Inspirational Endeavors, LLC. Rodney's mission is to serve as an example that will inspire, motivate, and encourage others to never give up, but instead reach for their hopes and dreams with earnest expectations regardless of their current limitations or challenges. His purpose in life is to "make a positive impact on the lives of millions of others", which he accomplishes via his books, digital programs, mentoring programs, tele-seminars, speaking engagements and by helping others overcome challenges and obstacles, so they can live joyfully with purpose and realize their dreams. His work has been endorsed by Bob Proctor, Peggy McCall, and many others.

He's been featured on multiple TV and radio platforms including The Nikki Rich Show, The Dr. Stem Show, as well as Get Bold Today hosted by multiple Emmy-winner LeGrande Green. Rodney is also an active member of the Power Your Life Network.

After a traumatic high-school football injury in 1993, he was bound to the confines of his wheelchair. Although Rodney was told his recovery prognosis was unfavorable, he knew he would turn things around, make an impact on the world, and walk again. With self-determination and faith in his ability to persevere, he did!

Rodney Flowers is the author of the life-affirming and highly-inspiring Amazon bestselling book, *Get Up! I Can't. I Will. I Did . . . Here's How!* which teaches empowering life principles to transform your spirit and motivate you to awaken the amazing power within you to overcome any challenge. He also authored the international bestselling book, *Essential Assertions,* packed with guiding life principles & inspiring stories that energize and motivate you to recognize your maximum potential, uncover and leverage your hidden strengths, & use your unbreakable spirit to capitalize on life's opportunities. Rodney's a co-author of the Amazon International Best-seller, *Unwavering Strength, Volume 2.*

To find resources and information that teach important life practices that assure you will always get back up when adversity strikes, visit www.RodneyFlowers.com.

Are you looking for answers?

Do you have a burning question that, if answered, will help you *Get Up and Achieve More* in life?

We're here to help!

Submit your questions to us

Send your questions to:

Rodney@RodneyFlowers.com

All questions submitted will be reviewed and may be considered for *Conversations with Rodney Volume II*.

Available for purchase on Amazon and Barnes & Noble

Get Up!
I Can't. I Will. I Did ... Here's How!

Essential Assertions
Unlocking the Power Within, Realizing Your Self-Empowered Potential, and Taking Advantage of Life's Opportunities

Unwavering Strength Volume 2
Stories to Warm Your Heart and Soul

Sign up for the Get Up and Achieve More Program

http://GetUpAndAchieveMore.com

To purchase or learn more about the other products and programs from international bestselling author Rodney C Flowers that will enable you to Get Up and Achieve More, please visit our store at http://www.RodneyFlowers.com/store.

Orange Get Up Tee

Blue Get Up Tee

Black Get Up Tee

www.ingramcontent.com/pod-product-compliance
Lightning Source LLC
LaVergne TN
LVHW011210080426
835508LV00007B/699